ROGER KAUFMAN
Philip GRISÉ

Auditing
Your Educational
Strategic Plan

Making a Good Thing Better

CORWIN PRESS, INC.
A Sage Publications Company
Thousand Oaks, California

For information address:

Corwin Press, Inc.
A Sage Publications Company
2455 Teller Road
Thousand Oaks, California 91320

SAGE Publications Ltd.
6 Bonhill Street
London EC2A 4PU
United Kingdom

SAGE Publications India Pvt. Ltd.
M-32 Market
Greater Kailash I
New Delhi 110 048 India

Printed in the United States of America

Library of Congress Cataloging-in-Publication Data

Kaufman, Roger A.
    Auditing your educational strategic plan : making a good thing better / Roger Kaufman, Philip Grisé.
        p.   cm.
    Includes bibliographical references.
    ISBN 0-8039-6299-1 (cloth) — ISBN 0-8039-6237-1 (pbk.)
    1. Educational planning—Auditing.   I. Grisé, Philip.   II. Title.
LC71.2.K38   1995
371.2′07—dc20   95-796

This book is printed on acid-free paper.

95 96 97 98 99   10 9 8 7 6 5 4 3 2 1

Corwin Press Production Editor: S. Marlene Head

Contents

About the Authors   vii

1 Introduction: Why Audit a Strategic Plan?   1

2 The Basics of Strategic Planning   3

   2.1 Six Critical Success Factors   3

      A. Moving Out of Your Comfort Zone   3
      B. Differentiating Between Ends and Means   5
      C. Using and Integrating Results   7
      D. Preparing Objectives   8
      E. Defining "Need"   10
      F. Planning Based on Your Ideal Vision   12

   2.2 The Organizational Elements Model (OEM)   19

      A. Outcomes   19
      B. Outputs   21
      C. Products   22
      D. Processes   22
      E. Inputs   23

   2.3 Costs-Consequences Analysis   23

      A. Linking Consequences   24
      B. Defining the Costs-Consequences Dimension   24

3 Building an Integrated Framework   26

   3.1 Describing the Integrated Framework   26

      A. Strategic Planning Plus (SP+)   27
      B. Results, Consequences, and Payoffs   30

3.2 The Three Stages of Strategic Planning Plus   30

    A. Scoping   30
    B. Planning   36
    C. Implementation and Continuous Improvement
       (Evaluation)   38

4 **Avoiding Common Mistakes**   **43**

5 **The Audit**   **46**

5.1 The Scope of the Strategic Plan   46

    A. The (Ideal) Vision   46
    B. Measurability of the Ideal Vision   50
    C. Level and Scope of Strategic Planning   53
    D. The Planning Partnership   60
    E. Aligning Beliefs and Values   61
    F. Needs Assessment and Identification   62
    G. Identifying the Current Mission   71

5.2 Planning   73

    A. Identifying Strengths, Weaknesses, Opportunities,
       and Threats (SWOTs)   73
    B. Selecting Long- and Short-Term Missions   74
    C. Deriving Decision Rules (Policies)   75
    D. Developing Your Strategic Plan   75
    E. Implementation and Continuous Improvement   76
    F. Determining Met/Unmet Objectives   77
    Summary   77

Appendix A: Scoring Table   78

Appendix B: A Calibration of Your Progress   86

Appendix C: Glossary of Terms   87

References and Suggested Readings   91

About the Authors

Roger Kaufman is Professor of Educational Research and Director of the Center for Needs Assessment and Planning at Florida State University. He is also affiliated with the faculty of Industrial Engineering and Management Systems at the University of Central Florida. He has served as a Professor at the United States International University and at Chapman University, both in California. He has also taught at the University of Southern California and Pepperdine University. He earned his Ph.D. (communications) from New York University, an M.A. (psychology and industrial engineering) from Johns Hopkins University, and a B.A. (psychology, sociology, and statistics) from George Washington University.

In addition, he has held positions in the private sector, including Boeing, the Martin Company, US Industries, and Douglas Aircraft. His consulting clients include educational systems, governments, and corporations in the United States, Canada, Latin America, Europe, New Zealand, and Australia. He is a Fellow in Educational Psychology of the American Psychological Association and a Diplomate in School Psychology of the American Board of Professional Psychology. He has been named "Member for Life"—their highest honor—by the National Society for Performance and Instruction, an organization in which he served as president. He was the 1983 Haydn Williams Fellow at the Curtin University of Technology in Perth, Australia. He has published 29 books on strategic planning, quality management and continuous improvement, needs assessment, management, and evaluation and is the author of more than 150 articles on those topics.

Philip Grisé is the Associate Director for the Center for Needs Assessment and Planning at Florida State University. For the past 10 years he has served as principal investigator on a variety of research projects that explore the impact of educational and community programs as individuals transition into society. These include work with alternative education scenarios for "at-risk" students, adult and community education programs, the GED, programs for the disabled, and inmate education programs. His Ph.D. and M.S. degrees were granted by Florida State University in the early 1970s in the field of educational research. His baccalaureate was earned from American International College in Springfield, Massachusetts in psychology, with a minor in education. For more than a decade, he designed, developed, and coordinated the state of Florida's assessment programs for the disabled and adults. He also established alternative assessment techniques and modifications that enable disabled persons to demonstrate performance through traditional competency-based assessment instruments.

Grisé has been the principal author on scores of research reports and has published several articles on adult and alternative education. He authored, with Donna Crowley, a computer software program to teach reading comprehension skills to hearing-impaired youth, which was named an award winner by the Johns Hopkins National Search for Computing Applications to Assist Persons With Disabilities. He has made numerous presentations at regional and national conferences and chaired or co-chaired four national meetings on testing or at-risk student issues. He also serves as the adult education resource person for Florida's Educational Reform and Accountability Commission.

1

Introduction:
Why Audit a Strategic Plan?

A strategic planning audit can be good for your educational health. Although most people think of an audit as something bad—what an adversary evokes in order to bring harm—we in no way have this concept in mind. The following is meant for your own use in order to find out what you now have in place. It is self-help in the best sense. What would you do well to continue, and what might you add, modify, or even stop? Rather than wait for a bad (or good) event to happen, you can begin to assess your situation right now—just you and your educational partners.

An audit helps you to be a successful educator, assisting you in checking your current strategic plan. How might you improve or transition from a system facing hard times, possibly even destruction (e.g., Marshall & Tucker, 1992; Kaufman, 1992c, 1995)? The audit in this book points the way to the results you and your community want, require, and deserve.

First, we define why you should do an audit (or review) of your strategizing. Next, we define and explain educational strategic planning, and then present the audit itself.

It is true: Failing to plan is planning to fail. We agree with Bob Mager's (1975) advice that if we don't know where we are headed, we might end up someplace else. In addition to this sage thought, we have also found it necessary to have full confidence that we are moving in the correct direction. Strategic plans tell us where to head, why to go, and what functions and resources it takes to get from here to there. They reveal our destinations so we can identify the most efficient and effective ways to proceed.

Many educational agencies have executed a so-called strategic plan, but most are disappointed with the consequences. What starts off with enthusiasm quickly turns to drudgery, lethargy, and, yes, even contempt for the process. It doesn't have to be so. We realize that there are a number of strategic planning approaches being used in education, and this book does not aim to show one as better than others. Rather, we identify the basic characteristics of successful strategic planning and allow you to determine which elements are already in your process and what might be added. Compare your approach and results with the basic criteria here, and you will know what to continue and what to change.

Now for some choices:

1. If you want the background for educational strategic planning so that the terms and concepts will be clear, go to Chapter 2.
2. If you have confidence in your knowledge of strategic planning, go directly to the audit in Chapter 5.

In either case, we supply a glossary of strategic planning and needs assessment terms in Appendix C. Appendix A contains a Scoring Table with which you can rate yourself on the comprehensiveness of your strategic planning efforts. Appendix B, A Calibration of Your Progress, has a series of bar graphs, one for each of the 10 major areas within the audit. You may enter your score for each section and determine—from a thumbnail sketch—how thoroughly you addressed each area.

2

The Basics of Strategic Planning

2.1 Six Critical Success Factors

The audit process described in this book is designed to help you define and deliver useful results. In the paragraphs that follow, we share some basic undergirding concepts. For a complete discussion, please review Kaufman's *Mapping Educational Success* (1995).

There are six critical success factors in strategic planning:

- Moving out of your comfort zone to reach useful destinations
- Differentiating between ends and means (what, not how)
- Using and integrating planning and results—Mega, Micro, Macro
- Preparing objectives that include measures of how to know when you have arrived (destination plus success criteria)
- Defining "need" as a gap between current and desired results
- Using an ideal vision as the underlying basis for planning.

A. Moving Out of Your Comfort Zone

Critical Success Factor 1: Move out of your comfort zone in order to define and reach useful destinations.

The first critical success factor—upon which all the others depend—encourages us to go beyond the known, the acceptable, and the conventional. If we do only what is comfortable, we risk

3

increasing our efficiency only in reaching outmoded, incomplete, or even wrong destinations. In a constantly changing world, old ground rules, boundaries, and frameworks threaten to steer us toward that to which Peter Drucker (1973) alerts us: getting better and better at doing what should not be done at all.

Fundamental, down-to-the-core changes in the way we think about education, as well as how we view the contributions and activities of educational partners in the public sector, are long overdue. Now is the time to consider doing what is right. Pushing on our current comfort zones by identifying new objectives will ultimately bring true success, that which is beyond the merely acceptable. As we extend ourselves past what is simply safe, we learn to define and deliver what is most useful. In the final analysis, this is actually the least risky path.

Joel Barker in his *The Business of Paradigms* (1989) and *Paradigm Pioneers* (1993) shows how formerly great enterprises, such as the Swiss watch behemoth, have suffered because they overlooked the presence of a paradigm shift. Their old boundaries and ground rules just didn't work anymore. In education, we have gone beyond many old concepts (i.e., all learning happens in classrooms, only teachers can deliver education, textbooks drive the curriculum, longer school days and years bring more learning, and only more money is required to get necessary results). Nevertheless, there are many items of conventional wisdom still under serious and necessary scrutiny (Kaufman, 1993c).

The importance of constantly reviewing frames of reference, even though a person has been successful so far, is discussed by several contemporary authors (e.g., Argyris, 1991; Barker, 1992; Drucker, 1993; Hammer & Stanton, 1995; Marshall & Tucker, 1992; Martin 1993). They suggest that the very approaches that have given an individual past success might be the ones leading to tomorrows' failures. In other words, the past is prologue. The future requires different paradigms and different planning approaches.

Futurists such as Toffler (1990) and Naisbitt and Aburdene (1990) remind us how much the world has changed. Meanwhile, policy experts such as Osborne and Gaebler (1992), and educational planners such as Kaufman (1992c, 1995; Kaufman, Herman, & Watters, 1995), reinforce the fact that education often suffers from backwards planning with an emphasis on dollars, resources, and processes. Successful and useful strategic planning mandates new missions, new needs, and new realities that are driven, instead, by well-defined outcomes.

B. Differentiating Between Ends and Means

Critical Success Factor 2: Differentiate between ends and means (focus on "what," not "how").

This second most important strategic success factor permeates everything in successful planning and thinking. Ends are results to be delivered; means are the resources and methods for delivering the results. Ends to be measured should be based on reality, not simply on things that are easy to capture. In addition, these results specifications should find common agreement among "hard" (performance) data as well as "soft" (judgment) data, both focused on ends-oriented perceptions. Planning that starts with means before identifying correct ends encourages us to develop and apply some very neat solutions that don't necessarily go with any known problems.

Strategic planning objectives should target ends—the results we want to accomplish. Indeed, the only sensible way to select a means, solution, resource, or "how-to-do-it" is on the basis of the results and payoffs we intend to deliver.

How to tell if you are ends-oriented. For each objective you develop, ask the following: "If I did this, or accomplished it, what result (and payoff) would I get?" The answer identifies an end when it targets a result, consequence, or impact. The answer focuses on a means when it targets resources (money, teachers, administrators, equipment, facilities) and/or methods (accelerative learning, human resources developing, planning, total quality managing, benchmarking). Figure 2.1 provides an aid to help assure that your planning statement will focus on results.

For example, suppose someone set this objective: We will begin the development of a course for using computers in introductory biology. The first question in Figure 2.1 helps us realize that "developing" (like most words ending in "ing") is a means, not an end. We then branch and confront whether or not we can differentiate between ends and means. If we can, then we ask: If I did develop and deliver a computer-driven course on introductory biology, what results should I get?

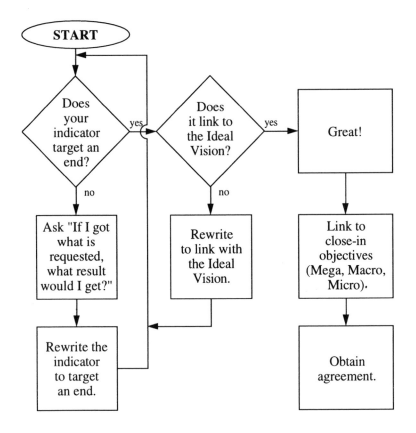

Figure 2.1. An Algorithm for Linking Indicators to an Ideal Vision, and Then to the Other Levels of Planning, to Help Achieve a Useful and Common Set of Results

By closely examining our means (computer-driven course) to define desired ends, we might realize even more. For instance, we might want learners to demonstrate knowledge of the basics of biology and be able to apply them, including, for example, the composition of human and plant cells and the methods of reproduction. Furthermore, we may want learners to score above the national average in science on the SAT and be accepted with advanced standing in accrediting colleges.

This "press" into results would transform our intention: By June 1, at least 95% of the learners will successfully demonstrate their knowledge of the following biological facts and their ability to apply them as certified by the instructor of record using valid applications assessments; and the next time these learners take the SAT, at least 80% will score above the national average on science. The foregoing statement targets ends, not just the means of a solution or intervention—the computer-driven course. As a result of the ends/means analysis, we might select still other means, perhaps video disks, internships, programmed texts, or peer tutoring.

How often do we jump right into a means (reforming curriculum, adding police officers to halls and playgrounds, HRD, inservice training, planning, communicating, meeting) without clearly defining the results and payoffs to be delivered? A focus on ends will stop the enemy of selecting solutions that don't go with our problems and thereby limiting opportunities that might otherwise be available.

C. Using and Integrating Results

Critical Success Factor 3: Use and integrate all three levels of results—Mega, Macro, Micro.

It is best to assure that the ends and means at each level of planning—Mega, Macro, and Micro—not only relate with each other but also integrate with the other levels in order to reap positive and important societal/client payoffs. The three levels of planning and results are as follows:

Level of Planning	Primary Client and Beneficiary
Mega	Society and Community
Macro	Educational Organization (itself)
Micro	Individuals and/or Small Groups

Every organization is made up of interacting parts with a common purpose. By recognizing this critical success factor, you will encourage a creative synergy in your organization. As an example, imagine you are a school dietitian. You are to develop a menu for each day so that the cooks know what to prepare. Here are the three levels of results you could link. (Remember that cooking is a means, and so are the ingredients you might use.)

Daily menu: Micro-level result

Nutritious diet: Macro-level result

Student/employee health and physical well-being: Mega level result.

If we prepare a menu without relating it to being a part of a nutritious diet, and if that weren't linked to the clients' health and well-being, we might end up with food that didn't contribute to lowering illness, reducing insurance premiums, and contributing to more vitality and readiness for learning and teaching.

We can identify and relate the three levels of results by asking ourselves this: When I get this result, what level will it affect? What question (Table 3.2) will it answer? If the result will improve competence and performance at the learner performance "building-block" level (a quality instructional module, a report that is accepted by one's supervisor), then it complements the Micro level. Next ask: Will this contribute to supporting the Macro-level question? The Mega-level question? If the links are not there, the result probably has little or no organizational or societal value.

Figure 2.2 provides an algorithm for sorting out vertical building-block possibilities. If what you deliver has no ultimate contribution to the external client (leading toward good citizenship, encouraging self-reliance, creating a safe environment), then this result is a prime candidate to be eliminated.

D. Preparing Objectives

Critical Success Factor 4: Prepare objectives—including mission objectives—that incorporate measures of how you will know you have arrived (statement of destination plus success criteria).

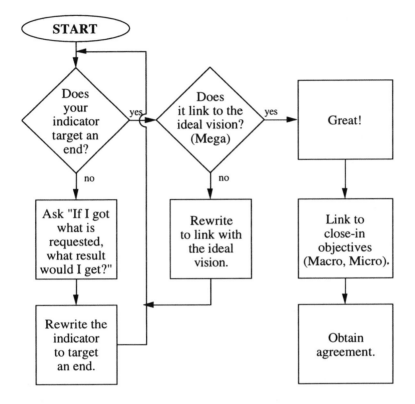

Figure 2.2. An Algorithm for Assuring Your Results Link at All Three Levels

To make a practical strategic plan, you will want more than a results-oriented perspective and knowledge of the three levels of results. In fact, whenever you write an objective at the Mega, Macro, and Micro levels of planning, it should have the following elements:

1. What result is to be accomplished?
2. Who or what will demonstrate the accomplishment?
3. Under what conditions will the accomplishment be observed?

4. What measurable criteria will be used to determine the accomplishment?

Table 2.1 provides a format for preparing useful objectives.

Avoid "how-to-do-it"s—methods, means, resources—in an objective. Even if you have been taught to write objectives, pay particular attention to the ends, or results. One flaw in current objective writing is including "how" the objective will be met (using computer-assisted instruction, applying current adult learning principles, tapping counseling department resources) before, or even without, defining the results to be delivered. Selecting "how" before knowing "what" is wasteful and violates Critical Success Factor 2.

A useful declaration of organizational purpose begins with a *mission objective* that is specific about where it is headed *and* how to tell when it has arrived:

MISSION STATEMENT + MEASURABLE CRITERIA = MISSION OBJECTIVE

A mission objective, like any other objective, provides direction and destination—the two often forgotten "D"s. For example, "quality in everything we do" is motivational, but it doesn't let you or anyone else know (1) what criteria we will use to measure quality, and (2) what is included in "everything." Add the criteria for success, such as the following: Our organization will win a Department of Education excellence in education award within two years; increase graduation rates to at least 99% of entering learners, and have at least 98% of all graduates get a job or enter an accredited higher education program.

E. Defining "Need"

Critical Success Factor 5: Define "need" as a gap between current and desired results (not as insufficient levels of resources, means, or methods).

When we care more about results than means, more about "what" than "how," when we define success in terms of accom-

TABLE 2.1. The ABCD Format for Preparing Useful Objectives (from Kaufman, 1992c, 1995)

A Format for Preparing Measurable Objectives: As Easy as ABCD

ABCD Element	Hypothetical Objective
A: Who or what is the Audience, target, or recipient?	100% of all learners, completers, and leavers who enrolled at the English-Steffy Unified School District after September 1, 1998.
B: What Behavior, performance, accomplishment, end, or result is to be demonstrated?	Will be accepted to postsecondary education, and/or get and keep a job that pays at least as much as it costs them to live. None will drop out without meeting state requirements, and all will be self-sufficient.
C: Under what Conditions will the behavior or accomplishment be observed?	Both in school and beyond exit: Each year, there will be an independent audit of in-school registrations and district records, as well as an independent placement and follow-up study of all completers and leavers.
D: What Data--criteria, ideally measured on an interval or ratio scale--will be used to calibrate success?	There will be 0 unapproved dropouts, and 0 previously enrolled learners who did not get accepted to a postsecondary program accredited by a regional education commision and/or who did not get and keep a job for at least 6 months (barring seasonal or economic layoffs) as reported and certified by the superintendent.

11

plishments and contributions, not on effort or expenditures, then we are using "need" to signify the gaps between current and desired results. When doing a "needs assessment," we define and prioritize the gaps between our current results and payoffs and the ones we desire. On the other hand, to use "need" as a verb—like most other English words ending in "ing"—is to see it as a means; that is, to prescribe solutions (such as teaching, or even strategic planning) that might not meet the needs or close gaps in results.

F. Planning Based on Your Ideal Vision

Critical Success Factor 6: Use an ideal vision as the underlying basis for planning (don't limit yourself to your organization).

Plans must have a destination. If plans use only today's realities, we won't even think to develop a new reality. Exclusively using current frames of reference can lock us into "acceptable educational solutions"—successful or not. This critical success factor asks us to override fears and apprehensions and freely envision new vistas.

An ideal vision provides an ultimate destination, not just for one's own organization (a means to societal ends) but primarily for defining and achieving the kind of world we want for tomorrow's child. Although realizing that our ideal may never be fully accomplished, we will at least know the direction of our first steps and the nature of our commitment for the future (see Figure 2.3). We don't promise to get to the ideal vision, but it becomes a "guiding star" to which we relate our interim objectives, in step-ladder fashion, toward the ultimate destination.

Martin Luther King Jr. had a dream. Walt Disney said that if we can dream it, we can achieve it. The New Testament advises us that without a vision the people will perish. Without a distant dream—an ideal vision—we limit ourselves to the here-and-now, to self-fulfilling prophecies of minor gains, or possibly to the lowest common denominator. World competitiveness and mutual contribution, everyone being successful in life and in work, real quality of life, and environmental and personal safety depend on an ideal vision.

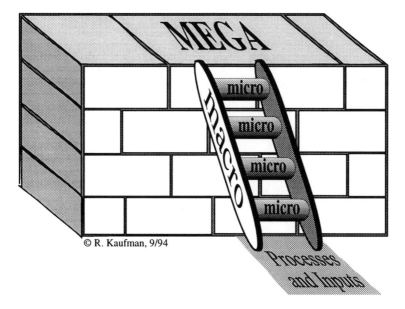

© R. Kaufman, 9/94

Figure 2.3. An Ideal Vision Serves as a Destination on a Far Horizon

Creating an ideal vision. Table 2.2 indicates a format for deriving a shared ideal future. It is important that Critical Success Factors 1, 2, 3, and 4 be observed in your definition.

It is generally fastest and easiest to use a generic ideal vision (such as the one provided here), asking your educational partners to react to it. After examining the sample you give them, including measurable criteria, they might add, delete, and/or modify what is provided. In setting criteria, there initially may be considerable philosophical argument ("What constitutes a murder?"), often focused on means rather than ends. For example, one might define murder as "the taking of another's life without that person's approval or overt contribution to this loss." This would foreclose inappropriate diversions into matters of culpability, such as discussing the *fault* of a 50-year-old ferry boat that was obviously listing to one side, claiming it murdered 312 people. In other words, did passengers boarding the ferry know that it might be unsafe?

TABLE 2.2 Format for Preparing an Ideal Vision and Useful Objectives

Describe the World in Which You and Your Partners Want Tomorrow's Child to Live
List the Criteria That Will Determine Your Progress and Success

Examples of ideal visions. The first one has been derived for a large nation/state:

> The world will be at peace, with no murder, rape, starvation, crime, or substance abuse that causes death or disabilities. All citizens will feel and be secure, moving around (the state) safely without regard to time or place. The world will be free of infectious disease, and every child brought into the world will be a wanted child. Poverty will no longer exist, and every woman and man will earn at least as much as it costs to live, unless moving toward becoming self-sufficient and self-reliant—no adult will be under the care, custody, or control of another person, agency, or substance. The unlucky and unfortunate among us will be helped to help themselves so that they are increasingly close to being and will become self-sufficient and self-reliant. People will take charge of their lives and be responsible for what they use, do, and contribute. Personal, intimate, and loving partnerships will form and sustain themselves.

No species will unintentionally go extinct due to human intervention, pollution, or action. Beaches, cities, towns, and the countryside will be free of litter, graffiti, and defacement. Accidents will increasingly approach and reach zero, and will not result in death, disability, or reduction of levels in daily living.

Government will contribute by assisting people to be happy and self-sustaining, reinforcing independence and mutual contribution. It will be organized and funded to the extent that it meets its objectives. State and business enterprises will earn a profit without bringing harm to their clients and our world.

The following paragraphs add measurable criteria to the above ideal vision using typical indicators as examples. Actual data must be valid and reliable. By requiring a criterion result to be "certified" as correct by a legitimate agent or agency, the state holds representatives accountable to use reliable and valid data—they will neither approve nor release anything without assuring its correctness. The appropriate valid and reliable data will be stated in the ideal vision with terms such as "as indicated by" or "as measured by":

The world will be at peace with neither loss of life nor wounded and disabled from declared or undeclared wars (as certified by the United Nations). There will be no murder, rape, crime, starvation, or substance abuse (as certified by the state attorney general and/or Department of Health and Human Services [HHS]). All citizens will feel and be secure, moving around the state safely without regard to time or place (indicated by a zero rate of personal assault, as certified by the attorney general).

The world will be free of infectious disease (as certified by the Centers for Disease Control and Prevention and HHS), and every child brought into the world will be a wanted child (as indicated by there being no child living below the poverty level as certified by HHS). Each individual's contribution will be at least equal to or greater than his or her consumption (as certified by the Department of Labor), and there will be zero convictions for child abuse (as certified by the national and/or state HHS). Poverty will not exist, and every woman and man will earn as much as it costs to live, unless preparing to be self-sufficient and self-reliant, and not under the care, custody, or control of another person, agency, or substance (as certified by the national and/or state HHS, and/or the Department of Labor or any other valid data base).

The unlucky and unfortunate among us will be helped to help themselves so they are increasingly close to, and ultimately become, self-sufficient and self-reliant (as indicated by an increase in life expectancy for these people and an increase in the amount of money their work produces and contributes to their subsistence, as certified by the national or state Department of Labor).

People will take charge of their lives and be responsible for their choices concerning what they use, do, and contribute (as indicated by no incarcerations or personal abuse of others and of substances, and by 100% voter registration and all voters participating at least once every 2 years (as certified by the attorney general or Department of Justice). Personal, intimate, and loving partnerships will form and sustain themselves (as indicated by a zero divorce rate and no judgments of physical abuse for persons living together as certified by the national or state HHS).

No species will unintentionally go extinct from human causes (as verified by the Department of Environmental Regulation [DER]), and there will be no death or disability from accident (as certified by the Department of Transportation or the Department of Highway Safety). Government's primary contribution will be assisting people to be happy and self-sustaining, and it will reinforce and achieve mutual contribution. It will be funded to the extent that it meets its objectives (as indicated by funding levels and Mega results referenced by agency budgets and evaluations, as certified by an independent, credible tax watch organization). Business will earn a profit without bringing harm to its clients and our mutual world (as certified by the Departments of Commerce and the Interior, along with the HHS).

From a different, noneducational, perspective, here is an ideal vision—without performance indicators yet added—for a health-related state agency:

Our citizens have a bright future. People take charge of their lives, become and remain healthy and self-sufficient. Families are strong, self-reliant, and productive. Neighborhoods are safe, supportive, and prosperous, with each resident contributing to the community and everyone in it.

This vision will become real as we trust people, as we earn the public's trust through our own excellence and contribution, and as we are full partners with people, families, and neighborhoods in their continuous improvement toward this ideal vision (based on Kaufman, 1995).

The next example of an ideal vision—with performance indicators—is for an educational agency:

The world will be at peace (as certified by the United Nations), and there will be no murder, rape, crime, or substance abuse (as certified by the Department of Justice). It will be free of death- or disability-causing infectious disease (as certified by the Centers for Disease Control and Prevention), and every child brought into the world will be a wanted child (as indicated by no child living below the poverty level and zero child abuse convictions, and so on, as certified by the HHS). Poverty will not exist, and every woman and man will earn at least as much as it costs to live unless preparing to be self-sufficient and self-reliant (as certified by the Department of Labor).

The unlucky and unfortunate will be helped to help themselves so they are increasingly close to, and ultimately become, self-sufficient and self-reliant (as indicated by an increase in life expectancy and in the amount of money their work produces and contributes to their subsistence, as certified by HHS and the Department of Labor).

People will take charge of their lives and be responsible for what they use, do, and contribute (as indicated by no incarcerations, no personal abuse of others, and the like, as certified by the Department of Justice). Personal, caring, and loving partnerships will form and sustain themselves (as indicated by a zero divorce rate, no judgments of physical or psychological abuse for persons living together, and so on).

Government's primary role will be contributing to all citizens who will become self-sustaining. It will reinforce independence and mutual contribution, being organized and funded to the extent that it meets its objectives (as indicated by funding levels and Mega results referenced by agency budgets and evaluations). Business will earn a profit without bringing harm to its clients and our world (as certified by the Departments of Interior, Commerce, and HHS) (based on Kaufman, 1995).

More alike than different. Ideal visions, because they speak to a preferred future, or "perfect world" (Senge, 1990), have much in common even though derived independently, as you have just observed above. The ideal vision for a pharmaceutical multinational may be quite similar to one for a school district—both identifying the kind of world in which they wish tomorrow's child to live. The similarities of elements and concepts stem from (1) an emphasis on ends and not means and (2) thinking in terms of the kind of world wanted for tomorrow's child.

The successful ideal vision also includes measurable criteria, as shown in the above examples and described in Critical Success Factor 4. Anything derived from this ideal vision statement can then be calibrated and partners can measure an organization's success.

Expanding ideal visions. Ideal visions should extend beyond the organization and target societal conditions and payoffs. It is a matter of overcoming conventional wisdom: Most ideal visions, we suggest, do not "reach" far enough, and they limit themselves to the educational agency. Ideal visions, as suggested in Critical Success Factor 6, should target societal requirements and not just the educational organization.

2.2 The Organizational Elements Model (OEM)

The OEM is a detailed framework for relating what Organizational Elements Model organizations—including educational ones—use, do, deliver, and accomplish. Every organization shares many similarities with others. Each uses ingredients, or inputs, that it forms and shapes into something tangible—products (courses passed, tests passed, and the like) and/or services delivered (completed learner counseling, registration). Then, organizations combine these "tangibles" into something they can deliver to external clients (graduates or completers). Finally, the success of the organization depends upon client satisfaction and the usefulness of what was delivered (getting and keeping jobs, self-sufficient citizens). (For a detailed discussion on the uses and applications of the OEM, see Kaufman, 1988c, 1992c, 1995; Kaufman et al., 1995; Kaufman & Zahn, 1993.)

Specific labels for these elements allow us to differentiate among them and relate them. Table 2.3 shows the organizational elements, examples of each, and how they define what organizations use, do, and deliver.

Education involves all of the elements in Table 2.3, meshing and melding them to deliver client satisfaction and usefulness. An effective and efficient educational process includes five elements. Three of the elements relate to results (outcomes, outputs, products), one relates to methods (processes), and the other to resources (inputs).

A. Outcomes

After a learner leaves an educational system—completes, graduates, or gets certified—there are consequences in and for the community and society called outcomes. Outcomes are the vital result aspect of Mega-level results.

Outcomes (Mega-level results): Repeat customers satisfied with the outputs; safe power tools; and a computer system that helps achieve a profit for the client.

Educational outcomes are Mega-level results. They are on the order of parents satisfied with the quality of education; a learner

TABLE 2.3 The Organizational Elements Model (OEM)

ORGANIZATIONAL LEVEL	OUTCOMES (the contributions and consequences of outputs in and for society and the community)	OUTPUTS (the aggregated products of the system that are delivered or deliverable to society)	PRODUCTS (en route --building-block-- results)	PROCESSES (how-to's; means; methods; procedures)	INPUTS (resources, ingredients, starting conditions)
EXAMPLES	Self-sufficient, self-reliant, productive individual who is socially competent and effective, contributing to self and others; no addiction to others or to substances; financially independent; continued funding of agency; etc.	Graduates; completers; dropouts; job placements; certified licensees; etc.	Course completed; competency test passed; skill acquired; learner accomplishments; instructor accomplishments; etc.	Total quality management - continuous improvement; teaching; learner; in-service training, managing, accelerative learning; site-based managing; accountability; etc.	Existing personnel; identified needs, goals, objectives, policies, regulations, laws, money, values, and societal and community characteristics; current quality of life, learner entry characteristics, teacher competencies, buildings, equipment, etc.
CLUSTER	SOCIETAL RESULTS/CONSEQUENCES	ORGANIZATIONAL RESULTS		ORGANIZATIONAL EFFORTS	
SCOPE	EXTERNAL (Societal)	INTERNAL (Organizational)			
PLANNING LEVEL	MEGA	MACRO	MICRO		
PRIMARY CLIENT OR BENEFICIARY	SOCIETY/COMMUNITY	SCHOOL SYSTEM OR SCHOOL	INDIVIDUAL OR SMALL GROUP		
STRATEGIC PLANNING QUESTION	Do you care about the success of learners after they leave the educational system and are citizens?	Do you care about the quality -competence- of the completers and leavers when they leave the educational system?	Do you care about the specific skills, knowledges, attitudes, and abilities of the learners as they move from course to course, and level to level?		

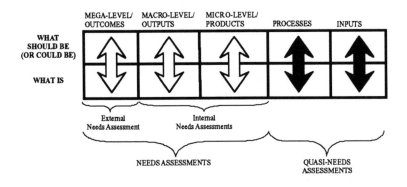

Figure 2.4. Three Varieties of Needs and Two Types of Quasi-Needs in Terms of the Organizational Elements Model (OEM)

who gets and keeps a job at or above the poverty level; or a graduate who enters and completes higher education.

The OEM is a useful tool, or template, for understanding what any educational organization uses, does, produces, and delivers. It will relate internal results—products and outputs—to external results called outcomes. If you examine what your system uses, does, and delivers and sort this information into the OEM, you can note what is missing. In this way you will observe how inputs, processes, products, outputs, and outcomes are (or are not) linked.

The OEM may be used as a two-tiered tool, with the dimensions of "what is" and "what should or could be" both displayed (see Figure 2.4). By entering what your organization uses, does, and delivers into this format, you may easily identify what is missing as well as what might be created.

B. Outputs

Remember, simply passing a course or winning a volleyball game doesn't make an educated individual or assure success in life. Higher order results, called outputs, now become important.

Outputs (Macro-level results): The results we can and do deliver to external clients. Outputs are the integration, the adding up, of all of the products; for example, a computer (made up of chips, disk drives, keyboard, cases, line cords) or a prescription drug (including bottle, packing cotton, pills, label, box).

All organizations, including educational systems, have outputs. Some examples are graduates from a vocational-technical high school, a certified licensed welder, and a merit scholar headed for our finest state university. We judge our educational outputs: we gather and report data on graduates, completers, noncompleters, job placements, college entries, and dropouts.

C. Products

Products are the Micro-level building-block results we get from the transformation of the inputs through application of our process.

Products (Micro-level results): Discrete results that contribute to other larger results.

In an educational agency, products might include a completed course, an instructional video, a correctly completed and filed attendance report, an accomplished guidance objective, a won softball game, an approved strategic plan, a passed literacy test, or a delivered art exhibit. Products in education are the building blocks of the system. Our curriculum specifies learning results that must be obtained (often noted in Carnegie Units). Educational products form the individual learner and teacher contributions. We often keep "score" on our products with grades and test results.

D. Processes

Processes: The methods and means used for getting things accomplished (activities, applied abilities, and skills); i.e., constructing and developing products, training and human resources development, personnel working, total quality management initiatives, and reengineering.

In an educational setting, processes include teaching learners, developing learning materials, scheduling activities (athletics, guidance and counseling, concerts, and performing arts), inservice training, and courses. Processes transform inputs into results. They should add value to the inputs in terms of the results they deliver

(Kaufman & Zahn, 1993). Processes are at the core of any educational enterprise. They are where we spend most of our time and commit most of our resources.

Inputs and processes are the factors of production, the ways and means by which education "gets done." They supply the ingredients for production and then transform the raw, or basic, materials into products.

E. Inputs

Inputs: Raw materials, existing facilities, and available resources; human capital; buildings and equipment; existing objectives, policies and procedures; and finances.

For educational systems, inputs include learners, teachers, values, schools, classrooms, media resources, available learning materials, budgets, board members, laws, board policies, preservice training levels and credentials, administrators, parents, community members, lobbyists, legislators, and the current perceptions of the schools— all of the ingredients used to do its work. Education deals with inputs that are different from those used for standard consumer products, such as automobiles and computers. Most important, learners bring with them a dazzling array of values, abilities, skills, and experiences.

2.3 Costs-Consequences Analysis

It is especially important in public sector programs to compare what gets put into a program with the value of what comes out. We must know the relationship between what resources are expended in making a program happen and what payoffs society receives in return for these efforts. Citizens, business professionals, educational administrators, politicians—everyone is paying attention to the consequences of spending time, money, and human resources in the form of actions.

Often we commit to a program and deliver it with enthusiasm and professional endeavor, without calibrating the extent to which our investment returns useful results. Sometimes, we don't even have useful indicators of the costs and consequences of our investments. Economists speak of a precise approach called "return on investment," a fine-grained determination of what costs are allocated to an intervention as compared to what the intervention delivers. Although this type of analysis may be desirable, decision makers often take a less detailed approach when wanting simply to explore the broad relationship between costs and consequences, between investments and payoffs. As an alternative, we have offered a straightforward method, costs-consequences analysis, using the OEM to consider the relationship between what is put into an intervention and what comes out—the value and worth of the contributions to the results attained.

A. Linking Consequences

The following portrays the types of relationships that link consequences with the OEM framework, giving you a variety of means by which to determine value and worth:

Auditing (or Accounting): a comparison of inputs to inputs

Cost-Efficiency Analysis: a comparison of costs to what is (or what will be) done and provided (means, methods, processes, procedures, interventions, activities, projects, and programs)—relating inputs to process

Cost-Effectiveness Analysis: relating costs to the achievement of products

Cost-Benefit Analysis: relating costs to outputs

Cost-Utility Analysis: relating costs to outcomes

B. Defining the Costs-Consequences Dimension

For each of the organizational elements used in the OEM table, there are numerous possible indicators. To understand the range of choices, we have provided examples in each category.

Outcomes: The societal consequences and payoffs for programs: self-sufficiency and self-reliance of participants in terms of income/personal expenditures; incidents and levels of government transfer payments; and remaining or becoming noninstitutionalized in jail or mental facilities—not under the care, custody, or control of another person, substance, or agency.

Outputs: Program completions, graduation, or certification; employment/nonemployment; and placements/nonplacements.

Products: The completion of activities, interventions, and program elements (including the performance requirements met).

Processes: The methods, means, and activities used with participants such as learners or teachers; the flow of people through the program(s) including the numbers and kinds of interventions.

Inputs: The numbers, kinds, and characteristics of people entering into programs; the criteria used for permitting entry; the numbers, kinds, and characteristics of program personnel; and the funds, organizational resources, laws, rules, regulations, and policies.

In addition, there are a number of questions that can be asked to help you plan a costs-consequences activity. A few of them are as follows:

- Who are the participants in the program(s)?
- Who are being turned down from program entry?
- What are the intervention programs participants are receiving?
- What are the results of the intervention(s)?
- What are the completion rates for participants?
- What are the job placement rates for completers (if relevant)? For the leavers?
- What is the societal condition of the completers? The noncompleters?
- What are the payoffs for various interventions for the various kinds of participants?
- What are the costs for the payoffs and nonpayoffs, and is it worth the expenditures as compared to what other possible interventions or programs, projects, or investments might be made?

3

Building an
Integrated Framework

3.1 Describing the Integrated Framework

The strategic planning approach used to prepare the audit in this book is based in part on Kaufman's work (e.g., 1992c, 1995; Kaufman et al., 1995), which incorporates the six critical success factors in decision making at all educational levels. Having been subjected to continuous improvement based on operational applications and performance information, this pragmatic framework has successfully affected public and private sector organizations worldwide—from the United States to Australia, from England to Chile. It makes possible a paradigm shift (Barker, 1989, 1992, 1993) because it challenges the comfort zones of those who would rather continue doing what they are currently doing, the way they are now doing it.

The strategic planning framework indicates a number of functions, or steps, for how to proceed with an audit—a process for defining useful (along with new and additional) objectives that are linked to effective and efficient tactics. It is organized into three major clusters:

- Scoping
- Planning
- Implementation and continuous improvement (evaluation)

The first step (see Figure 3.1) requires a decision concerning the primary focus or frame of reference that will be used: Who is the primary client and beneficiary of what gets planned and delivered?

There are three possible client groups educational planners might select: (1) the community and society that is being served, (2) the organization itself, and (3) individuals or small groupings (desired course results, student test results, academic departments, parent groups, the school board).

By first naming desired societal payoffs (healthy, self-sufficient, and self-reliant citizens; safe environment; business) that legally and ethically prosper, sensible decisions about curriculum, content, and methodology may be made. *Practical* strategic planning targets the current and future well-being of one's community and society—Mega-level results—as the safest choice for a primary client. There is, after all, abundant life after educational delivery.

Any strategic plan requires a tangible and useful purpose. The menu of questions that an educational organization should address is shown in Table 3.1.

A. Strategic Planning Plus (SP+)

When the Mega level is included in strategic planning, it becomes strategic planning plus (Kaufman, 1992c, 1995) or SP+. Mega-level planning incorporates Micro and Macro planning, aligning, and integrating of three levels to increase the likelihood of achieving organizational success. By proceeding in this way, with the Macro and Micro levels nested within the Mega level, there will be a linking and synergy among all elements, actions, and activities of the organization. This approach also avoids a narrow linear, or lock-step, process in favor of a dynamic, interactive human-centered one.

Table 3.2 demonstrates the relationship among levels of planning, types of persons who champion each level, and types of results delivered. In conventional terms, a leader might be the superintendent or board chair, the executive might a principal, and the supervisor/manager a department chair or program coordinator. Note that in our definition, anyone may become a leader while looking after the good of others, both those inside and those

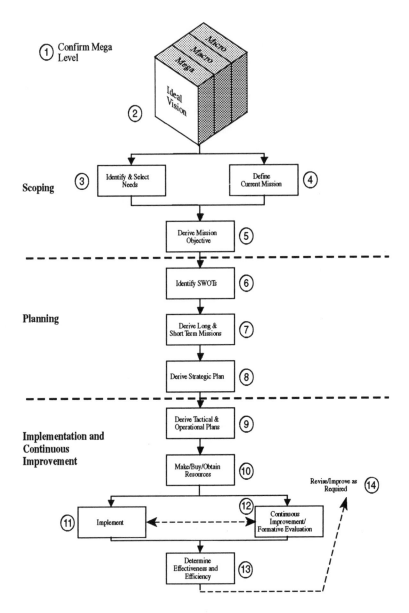

Figure 3.1. A Strategic Planning Framework Using Three Clusters—Scoping, Planning, and Implementation and Continuous Improvement (from Kaufman, 1995)

TABLE 3.1 Basic Questions an Educational Agency Should Ask and Answer (based on Kaufman, 1992c, 1995)

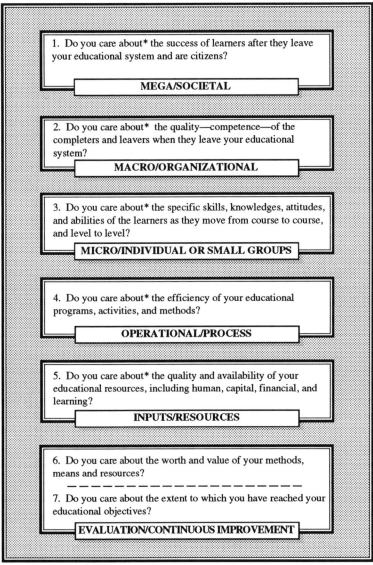

1. Do you care about* the success of learners after they leave your educational system and are citizens?

MEGA/SOCIETAL

2. Do you care about* the quality—competence—of the completers and leavers when they leave your educational system?

MACRO/ORGANIZATIONAL

3. Do you care about* the specific skills, knowledges, attitudes, and abilities of the learners as they move from course to course, and level to level?

MICRO/INDIVIDUAL OR SMALL GROUPS

4. Do you care about* the efficiency of your educational programs, activities, and methods?

OPERATIONAL/PROCESS

5. Do you care about* the quality and availability of your educational resources, including human, capital, financial, and learning?

INPUTS/RESOURCES

6. Do you care about the worth and value of your methods, means and resources?

7. Do you care about the extent to which you have reached your educational objectives?

EVALUATION/CONTINUOUS IMPROVEMENT

* and commit to deliver

TABLE 3.2 Planning, Personnel, and Results (based on Kaufman, 1993b)

Level of Planning	Type of Sponsor	Type of Result
Mega	Leader/Steward	Outcome
Macro	Executive	Output
Micro	Supervisor/Manager	Product

external to the organization. "Leader" here requires a formal consideration of the payoffs and usefulness of what the organization contributes to society. Thus "leadership" seems compatible with what Block (1993) calls "stewardship," although he seems to limit his discussion to the Macro level.

B. Results, Consequences, and Payoffs

This strategic planning process is results based and results centered as suggested by Critical Success Factor 2. Confusing means (how) and ends (what) will have profound implications on success—or lack of it. When resources and methods (means) are selected before relating them to the desired results (ends), one risks jumping into solutions without understanding the problems or opportunities. When one selects a means (longer school day, computer-assisted learning) before knowing the ends to be achieved, the results are almost always disappointing and expensive.

3.2 The Three Stages of Strategic Planning Plus

Referring to Figure 3.1, the following describes each of the three phases and its associated elements and suggests the sequence in which to proceed toward your goals.

A. Scoping

Step 1. Select the Mega-level scope of strategic planning from among three alternatives. This selection is based on who is to be the primary client and who benefits from what is planned and delivered—Mega, Macro, or Micro. Notice in Figure 3.1 that the Mega-level option includes Macro and Micro elements embedded within it. When you select Mega, you automatically get the others.

Warning: If you do not select the Mega level, you assume that positive societal consequences will surely flow. Failure to formally and directly target this level leaves an organization and everyone in it vulnerable to legitimate claims of selecting means and resources that cannot be justified. It is the Mega-level focus—SP+— that is unique within strategic planning approaches (Kaufman, 1992c, 1995), although more and more experts are now calling attention to the importance of a societal payoff (Drucker, 1992, 1993; Popcorn, 1991; Senge, 1990).

The Mega level is the most practical and pragmatic first choice because of this simple reality: Our educational organization is a means to societal ends. If education does not provide communities with safe, cost-effective, and cost-efficient learning plus mastery for students so they will be self-sufficient and self-reliant, not only today but also tomorrow, then all of our futures are threatened (e.g., Drucker, 1993; Marshall & Tucker, 1992; Naisbitt & Aburdene, 1990; Popcorn, 1991; Toffler, 1990). The current strident demands being placed upon educational agencies (that they be responsive and responsible) serve as testimony to the fact that we are not yet serving all learners in terms of becoming self-sufficient, self-reliant citizens and good neighbors.

Basic to selection at the Mega level is the development of a shared ideal vision. The building of, or agreeing on, this shared vision is an integral part of the first phase of strategic planning— the scoping process. The ideal vision is what defines the Mega level choice and commitment. As soon as the Mega choice is made, the next function is to identify the ideal vision.

Strategic planning is long-range planning that defines and continuously moves ever closer to the achievement of an ideal vision. At the scoping step, the planning partners identify and define "what should be" and "what could be" in terms of the ideal society.

Define the ideal vision. It is important to set an ideal vision first, *before* restricting oneself with "real-world" data. Issues of practicality should not be considered here, in order to encourage ourselves to go beyond what we believe we can achieve. If we don't reach for a better future through strategic planning, how will we ever (1) break out of the confines of our current paradigms and (2) know where to begin the journey?

An ideal vision should be related to contributions and consequences (ends), not to procedures, resources, or methods (means). Planning partners imagine a world in which they want their children and grandchildren to live and what they would like them to be partners in creating. If we want a peaceful world—no loss of life from armed hostilities, no deaths or disabilities from drug addiction, no requirement for welfare, no deaths or disabilities from crime, and no infectious disease to cause disability or loss of life—then high ideals benefiting all people should form the vision that is to become the organization's mission (see pp. 12-18).

The ideal vision should be developed by all those involved with the educational organization, both internally and externally. It is not a task left for the board or the superintendent. Instead, ownership is obtained from being an active participant in both the definition and realization of the ideal vision. As we move from having someone tell us what to do (conventional leadership) toward a shared commitment to a worthy future (stewardship), we increasingly recognize that the ideal vision contributes toward this end (see Block, 1993).

An ideal vision forms a basic framework through partnership relationships between organizations and associates, community members, governments, regulatory agencies, and business. By first selecting the part of the total ideal vision that the organization will deliver—the mission objective—the educational partners can subsequently identify what the other agencies and agents can contribute. Synergies among and between societal partners are therefore identified and delivered, thus creating the future rather than reacting to it.

An ideal vision is stated in terms of measurable performance. Although we might not achieve this objective in our lifetimes, we must set our compass to its ultimate destination. By making a firm commitment to the primary organizational mission (derived from the ideal vision), we discourage drift based on the status quo.

What about beliefs and values? Beliefs, values, and wishes all drive the ways in which partners address the strategic planning process. Without questioning their own private frames of reference, people usually apply their existing views about life, relationships, families, and neighbors to planning tasks. These unexamined and strongly held paradigms (sometimes referred to as "educational philosophy" or "core values") commonly focus on means and resources instead of results.

Deriving a shared ideal vision allows educational partners to compare their beliefs and values (often really only biases or stereotypes) with the kind of world we want for tomorrow's child. This process often helps partners effectively revise old patterns. The success of the entire strategic planning process might hinge on the planning partners' ability to consider new points of view about people, prejudice, education, business, government, health, and what the organization should accomplish.

Unfortunately, many popular strategic planning approaches begin with the naive view that "everyone's values are important and should be included," not taking into account that some values are antithetical to democracy, the dignity of human life, and the importance of helping all people to help themselves be successful. There are those who seek others to disproportionately shoulder their own share of contribution. In other words, they want—even demand—rights without appropriate responsibilities.

When one begins strategic planning with naked beliefs and values, processes, interventions, programs, how-to-do-its, and means ("use a systems approach," "drill and practice is good for the mind," "computer-assisted learning is dehumanizing," "all education should be home education," "teach humanism," "lengthen the educational day and calendar," "summer vacations are sacrosanct") are imposed before useful ends are identified and justified. Thus, with this premature starting point, organizations head off to do their work with solutions that do not fit the problems and opportunities.

An ideal vision that is cooperatively derived and shared facilitates partners in revising their current paradigms, even though this process frequently moves people outside of their comfort zones. Be patient as planning partners are challenged by letting go of long-held perceptions and allow them to grow, develop, and change. The results will pay handsomely in terms of what the educational organization will be able to contribute to our shared communities and society.

Step 2. Identify and define current mission. By doing Step 1 (above) and Step 3 (following) of this framework, the current mission is obtained and (as is usually necessary) rewritten in results terminology. These revisions are to include measurable indicators of "Where are we headed?" and "What criteria will allow us to tell when we have arrived?" Keep in mind that results-related objectives target only ends, never means.

Step 3. Identify needs. Using the definition of a "need" as a gap in results—Critical Success Factor 6—and employing both performance (hard data) and perception (soft data), the gaps between current results and desired results are identified (starting with the ideal vision). In Step 6 of this framework, we use this need data to identify gaps in results for closer-in years (2010, 2000, 1998, etc.).

The importance of conducting a needs assessment—the identification and prioritizing of needs that defines "need" as a gap between current and desired results—is basic and fundamental. To do otherwise permits means and resources to be selected without justifying them on the basis of getting from current results, payoffs, and consequences to desired ones (see Critical Success Factor 2).

Many so-called needs assessments, because they confuse ends and means, are really wish lists or solutions assessments. For example, an inservice needs assessment assumes that the solution is inservice training, thus focusing on training requirements before defining gaps in results for learners, community, and society. Actually, the term *training requirements analysis* is more appropriate here because training is a means that will not necessarily facilitate needs, a gap in results. In addition, the inclusion of both independently verifiable performance (hard) as well as personal observation (soft) data is vital in order to capture the full array of any gaps.

Needs are prioritized by assessing "What do you give?" as compared to "What do you get?" A needs assessment allows a decision to be made on the basis of what it costs to meet a need versus what it costs to ignore it.

An added bonus of considering "need" as a gap in results is that it then provides the basic criteria for evaluation and continuous improvement. In evaluation—the comparing of intentions with accomplishments—the "what should be" criteria are used for evaluation, eliminating the requirement of an independent evaluation and continuous improvement process.

Step 4. Identify the primary educational mission objective. At Step 4, the primary mission objective (including detailed performance criteria) is derived. It is based on the part of the ideal vision the educational agency commits to deliver and to continuously move toward. The mission objective is the basic direction in which your educational organization will head—the guiding star—and states the Macro-level results (outputs) to be delivered. The term *primary* is used only to emphasize that it is the basic objective from which all other mission objectives (for years spanning between now and the realization of this purpose) derive and relate.

Thus the primary mission objective is derived from the following: the ideal vision, the needs identified and selected, and the measurable definition of the current educational mission. When the needs have been identified at the ideal-vision level, educational planners estimate the costs versus results both for meeting and for not meeting these needs. From that, they can identify those elements of the ideal vision they will commit to deliver . . . the new mission objective.

In summary, the primary mission objective is based upon (a) the selection of the Mega level for strategic planning, (b) the derivation of a results-referenced ideal vision (reconciling any beliefs and values that have surfaced during its derivation), (c) identified needs, (d) costs-consequences (or cost-results) estimations based on what it costs to meet and not to meet the needs (cost being both financial and social), (e) the elements the organization commits to deliver, and (f) the existing mission (that, as is usually required, has been transformed into terminology describing measurable performance). Those who select a mission objective that is not derived from the Mega- or ideal-vision level severely risk their entire enterprise.

The primary mission objective is, pragmatically, based on a comparison between current intentions (the results-defined current mission) and desired results (based on the ideal vision and the meeting of priority needs) in order to define what it will take to get from "what is" to "what should be." The mission *objective* identifies only the measurable destination on an interval or ratio scale, assuming that everything (even if we merely name it) is measurable. By contrast, a mission *statement* identifies only intentions that are measurable on a nominal or ordinal scale. The taxonomy of measurement used here is based on four scales: nominal (ranking), ordinal (greater than, less than, or equal to), interval (equal scale distances and arbitrary zero point), and ratio (equal scale distances and known zero point). The principles stated above can also be expressed as

MISSION STATEMENT + INTERVAL/RATIO SCALE CRITERIA
= MISSION OBJECTIVE

The skills of preparing measurable performance indicators and writing mission objectives in terms of results at the appropriate (and selected) level are key (Kaufman, 1992c, 1995; Kaufman, Rojas, & Mayer, 1993; Mager, 1975).

B. Planning

The strategic plan is built on information generated from the products of the previously mentioned scoping elements.

Step 5. Identify SWOTs: Strengths, Weaknesses, Opportunities, and Threats. The unearthing of the organization's strengths, weaknesses, opportunities, and threats is usually accomplished as well as analyzed through both internal and external scanning (Kaufman & Herman, 1991; Kaufman et al., 1995). Future trends and opportunities are documented at this important step (see Drucker, 1993; Naisbitt & Aburdene, 1990; Toffler, 1990). Although many are tempted to examine only negative factors, the identification of positive opportunities that might otherwise remain obscured is also critical (Kaufman, 1992c, 1995). Still, to begin sensibly, an organization will first identify its mission. The determination of SWOTs then provides the optimal "realism" for the strategic planning process.

Step 6. Identify the long- and short-term missions. With the shared ideal vision, identified needs, primary mission objective, and SWOTs in mind, select the long- and short-term—building-block—mission objectives. These linked, en route objectives (from year 2010 to 2000, from 1998 to next year) contain measurable specifications for the organization in terms of outputs—what skills, knowledge, attitudes, and abilities learners will have when they exit the system. They will prepare a bridge between current results and the achievement of the primary mission objective.

Building-block mission objectives are based upon trend data in addition to what is currently known and possible. The SWOTs information (from Step 5) forms a database from which to determine the long- and short-term missions. As with all objectives, these are to be written in measurable performance terms. The ideal vision and its related "results ladder" defining intended accomplishments from today toward the ideal provides the basis for continuous improvement of the system and its components (Kaufman & Zahn, 1993).

The primary mission objective (derived in Step 4) along with the building-block missions identify the results that the organization commits to deliver. Step 6 thus identifies a measurable objective that is a clear statement of "where we are headed" plus "what criteria we will use to know when we have arrived" for both close-in and distant destinations.

Step 7. Develop the strategic plan. Based on the products from framework Steps 1-6, this step will answer the key questions: What? How? Who? When? Why? and Where?

However, reconciling differences among the planning partners might have to be done once again. Take time to make sure every part of the strategic plan is based upon the ideal vision, identified needs, the primary mission objective, and the associated long- and short-term missions. When disagreements occur, they are usually over means and not ends. The products of Steps 1-5 provide the common ground: results to be achieved. Use the previous data and information to negotiate doing what is right, not just what is acceptable.

At this step, the planning partners frequently also must collect new and different data, a task arising from the requirement to compare the original ideal vision with the existing mission as a way of adequately identifying and justifying the needs it intends to reduce or eliminate. Prudence here will protect those who deserve the most effective and efficient educational system possible—the learners.

Operational, or en route, milestone results (functions) for implementation are set, along with the selection from alternatives of tactics and approaches (methods-means) to be used. The functions may be arranged to form a management plan (mission profile) that identifies the results to be accomplished and the order in which they should be completed (Kaufman, 1992c, 1995; Kaufman et al., 1995).

Strategic plans should be neither long nor complex—10 pages is about right. Tactics and operational plans (based on strategic plans) may form a separate document. Another product of Step 7 is the derivation of decision rules, or results-referenced policies. Policies based on results to be accomplished are necessary so that all partners have the same "marching orders." These decision rules provide strategic objectives with measurable criteria, unlike so-called policies that are really only compliance guidelines. Take care that your compliance guidance is based upon validated results to be achieved.

C. Implementation and Continuous Improvement (Evaluation)

Step 8. Put the strategic plan to work. The activities and results of this last SP+ step include the following:

(a) *A tactical plan*—the defining and selecting of the best ways and means to deliver the results required in the strategic plan. The tactical plan includes specifications for designing methods, means, and resources, justifying what is to be accomplished and how it will be done on a costs-consequences basis. During this step, you may both identify what should be delivered through education as compared to other interventions or delivery agencies (job aids and redesign; assignment; hiring; departments of health, labor, and employment) as well as consider alternative tools, techniques, and packages.

(b) *An operational plan*—the tactical plan identifies the steps for how-to-do-its, including timelines for accomplishing each product and delivering it to where it has to be, when it has to be there. The operational plan defines the details of getting all the tactics (methods-means) delivered including (a) developing (or acquiring) resources, (b) implementing what has been planned, (c) conducting formative evaluation, and (d) revising as required while implementation is being carried out.

(c) *Implementation*—putting the plans to work and tracking progress in order to change what is not working and continuing what is.

It takes some time to attend to these implementation-and-continuous-improvement elements, but now all of the requirements will be justified on the basis of

An ideal vision that defines the world for tomorrow's child

Gaps in results (needs)

Priority needs to be reduced or eliminated

Mission objectives that identify the results to be accomplished to get from current results to the ever closer achievement of the ideal vision

Measurable performance specifications for functions (building-block results) against which alternative methods-means (including curriculum and instruction) may be considered and selected on the basis of a costs-consequences analysis

This last SP+ phase includes summative evaluation by which purposes (goals and objectives) are compared with results. Based upon the evaluation—comparing results with intentions—decisions are made about what to continue and what requires revision. In addition, the evaluation and continuous improvement criteria are taken directly from the "what should be" portion of the needs assessment.

Strategic planning is a continuing process, a way of thinking as well as a tool for deriving a formal plan. By taking a Mega-perspective, the linkages will be reflected throughout.

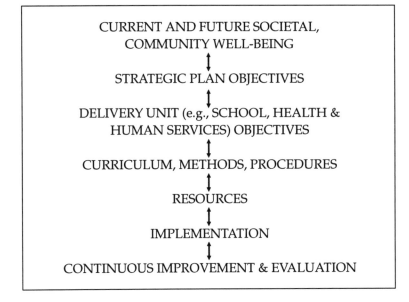

Implementing Strategic Planning Plus. Following are the steps for a proactive and holistic strategic planning plus (SP+) activity:

(a) Obtain board and executive commitment to Mega-level strategic planning.

(b) Obtain planning team commitment.

(c) Develop a shared ideal (Mega) vision. In doing this, the planning partners will have the opportunity to clarify, or even reconsider, their beliefs and values, including those related to change at all levels.

(d) Transform existing mission statement to a mission objective (where the system is headed and how to measure success).

(e) Identify needs—gaps in results—through comparing the ideal vision with current results and consequences.

(f) Prepare a primary mission objective for the entire educational organization.

(g) Identify strengths, weaknesses, opportunities, and threats (SWOTs) through internal and external scanning.

(h) Prepare building-block mission objectives for distant and closer-in results to be achieved in specified years in order to move continuously closer to the primary mission and the ideal vision.

(i) Derive functions and specific performance indicators required to meet the mission objective.

(j) Identify roles for accomplishing (f), (h), and (i).

(k) Identify and select ways and means to accomplish (f), as well as (h) and (i), including costs-consequences analyses.

(l) Manage implementation.

(m) Determine met and unmet objectives—based on the needs met and those still unmet, and revise and continuously improve as required.

Linking strategic plans to curriculum. It is best that curriculum be vertically integrated through the Micro, Macro, and Mega levels. To achieve this, the following steps should be applied. First, however, select an ideal vision along with an associated primary mission objective that clearly details which parts of the ideal vision the system is willing to help achieve:

(a) Conduct a needs assessment—identifying and prioritizing gaps between current results and desired ones—and place the needs in priority order. This will provide the greatest impact when begun at the Mega level; nevertheless, a needs assessment may be completed, in turn, for the Macro and Micro levels.

(b) Develop strategic objectives at the Mega (societal), Macro (organizational), and Micro (individual employee/learner) levels.

(c) Devise and implement a monitoring procedure that can maintain the quality level desired. This is done by ensuring that what is to be taught (curriculum) becomes what is actually taught (instruction), and what is assessed (mastery measurement) is observed. The objectives are the "what should be" dimensions of the needs selected for closure, including the measurable performance standards that form the objectives.

(d) Ensure vertical articulation of what is planned, taught, and learned so that the Mega, Macro, and Micro levels are achieved.

(e) Institute a quality management plus (QM+) process that assures continuous improvement of the entire system as it moves constantly toward the mission objective and the ideal vision.

(f) Design and develop learning materials and methods that will efficiently and effectively deliver mastery. The methods and techniques of instructional systems design and development are invaluable for this.

(g) Consider the use of a variety of alternative delivery methods and means (e.g., technologically driven methods such as distance and distributed education delivery) to motivate learners and to assure efficient delivery.

(h) Model, with your curriculum and instruction, what we want our learners to master and apply.

(i) Implement the curriculum, and conduct formative (en route) evaluation—changing that which is not successful, continuing that which is. Provide modified learning experiences for learners where the curriculum and instruction has not been effective.

(j) Evaluate the effectiveness and efficiency of the curriculum, deciding what to change and what to continue.

(k) Revise as required. Continuously improve as you move toward your mission objective and the ideal vision.

4

Avoiding Common Mistakes

Here is how to avoid the most frequent mistakes made by strategic planners and instructional developers. Circumventing errors others have made could mean the difference between developing just another document that gathers dust or creating a revitalized educational organization with responsive instruction and optimal learning opportunities.

1. Don't plan at the course or program level without first linking to the societal level. Educators are chartered to provide learners with the abilities to be successful contributing citizens and employees in a world that is rapidly changing. In this climate, our organizations must be responsive and responsible or they will cease to exist.

If we don't define future societal success and realities, then we assume what we do will be useful. How successful is our current organization from a societal perspective? Can it simply be patched and mended by adding a course here, tougher requirements there? To be successful, the three levels of results (Mega, Macro, and Micro) must also be vertically integrated.

2. Never prepare objectives in terms of means instead of results. Objectives tell us where to head and how to know when we have arrived. If we only set our sights on processes (using computers) or resources (higher spending), we put the course-methods cart before the expected-results horse. Objectives must identify ends, not means or resources.

3. Don't develop a plan without the input and cooperation of representative organizational and external partners. Although a plan might be put together more quickly when done by a small group, the product will not likely be accepted by others who haven't been able to contribute. When partners actually develop the plan, they ensure that it is better, representative, and adopted.

4. Never select solutions before identifying destinations. Just about every group, good or bad, has a favorite solution or quick fix. Resist picking a solution (or resource) until you know where you are headed and why.

5. Don't set objectives based solely upon the perceptions of the planning partners without also assuring that their percep-tions are anchored in performance realities. People typically know what they *want*, but they often don't know what they should *have*. They also don't know much about gaps between current results and required ones. Provide planning partners with the realities of future trends, opportunities, and consequences. By starting with a collection of core values, you risk "air hardening" outmoded frames of reference. By starting with the develop-ment—or modification—of an ideal vision, you allow the partners to grow, develop, and change.

6. Never define and identify needs as gaps in resources, meth-ods, or techniques. Although popular usage recognizes "need" as a verb ("we need more money," "we need more teachers"), this is a sure way to select solutions that really aren't responsive to the basic problems. If you first identify needs as gaps between current results and desired ones, you will be free to select the most efficient and effective ways to meet your needs.

7. Don't skip steps in the strategic planning process. Leaving out even one step will diminish the quality and usefulness of the strategic plan. Review the model (Figure 2.1) and the questions (Table 3.1). Which steps and questions can really be omitted?

8. **Don't assume that all strategic planning approaches are (a) basically the same, and/or (b) nothing but common sense/intuition.** All models are not the same. Most are reactive *and* start at too low a level. Many attempt to improve courses or increase graduation rates, not turn out learners who will be successful citizens. If intuition alone were enough, the field of education and your organization would be wonderful just as they are.

9. **Don't develop instructional programs on the basis of producing efficient delivery without questioning the validity and usefulness of the learning objectives.** Many improvement initiatives assume that the current objectives are correct and useful. They try to improve the efficiency of delivery and/or provide branching for the learner within the prescribed course content. However, we can make training more efficient without making it effective—both in school and in life.

10. **Don't fail to integrate strategic planning with other improvement initiatives such as quality management, needs assessment, and reengineering.** Although most organizations are appropriately moving into strategic planning and quality management (or total quality management), they may be splintering their efforts. Quality management and strategic planning use the same databases and also must involve all partners in their pursuit and accomplishment. Integrating these thrusts, including using the same partners, can better assure continuous improvement toward the mission and ideal vision.

11. **Don't move ahead incrementally instead of going directly to what has to be accomplished.** The conventional advice is to crawl before you walk, but the clock on educational survival is running. People will move out of their comfort zones as they realize that it is not only practical to do so (their survival depends on it, as noted by Conner, 1992) but also ethical (Kaufman & Watters, 1992). Knowing the right thing to do and deliver and not doing so is a breach of professionalism.

5

The Audit

This section of the book provides step-by-step details for assessing the usefulness and comprehensiveness of your strategic planning effort. By using the evaluative tools provided, you will develop a record of your strategic planning steps. In the spirit of "revise as required," you can make changes to this record for future planning efforts.

5.1 The Scope of the Strategic Plan

A. The (Ideal) Vision

This audit area, the first of three questions asked below, is about the selected level for your ideal vision.

What level of vision did you select?

1. Ideal/Mega
2. Macro
3. Micro
4. Process
5. Inputs/Resources
6. "Attainable/practical"/Mega

7. "Attainable/practical"/Macro
8. "Attainable/practical"/Micro
9. "Attainable/practical"/Process
10. "Attainable/practical"/Resources
11. No vision statement used

The analysis: Take your vision statement and subject it to the analysis above. Identify the extent to which (a) an ideal— societal/community level—destination is stated, and (b) a primary focus—Mega, Macro, Micro, processes, or inputs/resources—is targeted.

If an ideal vision has not been developed, identify whether an attainable/practical rationale ("We want to be real-world, not hypothetical and academic" or "We know there will be no more money in the future, why even get our hopes up?") is responsible. If there is such a basic assumptional "driver," then determine the primary focus: Macro, Micro, process, or input/ resources. If nothing has been labeled as a vision, probe to find out if one might have been developed but not formally reported.

The ideal vision is best developed for society and community, not for your educational agency alone. In order for your mission objective to be useful, it must make a measurable contribution in this regard or likely never link or integrate smoothly with the Mega level. In other words, it might not be reality linked.

What is the depth of your ideal vision?

Scoring: Use the Scoring Table (Appendix A), which is based on the importance of defining a useful "guiding star" toward which all educational partners may steer and contribute. Head to the wrong destination (limit your contribution to courses or the numbers of graduates) and everything else will likely falter. If the plan is only interested in serving the district or certain staff members, then how can it make a continuing contribution to helping learners become functioning citizens and good neighbors?

Revision recommendations: By starting below the Mega level—without basing the mission objective and all that follows on the selected portions of the ideal vision—the assumptions of societal contributions are tenuous at best. In addition, aiming only for what is attainable is denying your educational agency the challenge of helping create a much better world. Incorporating the Mega level ensures the satisfaction of contributing learners who will be self-sufficient, self-reliant individuals not under the care, custody, or control of another person, agency, or substance.

Is the ideal vision really prepared for the societal level? Is your ideal vision written for the kind of world you and the educational partners want for tomorrow's child?

Scoring: Turn to the Scoring Table (Appendix A) and evaluate your ideal vision. If you scored 50 points in this section, your strategic planning is right on target. If you are in the positive range with 20 points, you are better off than most. Add measurable criteria to increase your responsiveness. If you have a negative score, it is time to shift out of the comfort zones of inputs and processes and work at the Mega level.

Revision recommendations: Although it is conventional to prepare an ideal vision for one's organization, doing so will not assure alignment of your mission with external reality or positive consequences. Ask the planning partners to consider the results chain that links the Mega, Macro, and Micro levels. Further, show that any mission objective should be derived from the ideal vision.

Rethinking the scope and level of your vision. As was suggested above, have the planning partners rethink who is to be the primary client and beneficiary of what their plan delivers. Get them to review recent research and thinking about paradigms and paradigm shifts. Revisit the work of Barker (1989, 1992, 1993), Kaufman, (1992c, 1995), Naisbitt and Aburdene (1990), Osborne and Gaebler (1992), Popcorn (1991), Senge (1990), and Toffler (1990).

Using the "Basic Questions an Educational Agency Should Ask and Answer" (Table 3.1), address the following:

1. Which questions do you think your educational agency *and* any of your clients can afford *not* to address formally (without identifying and using measurable performance terms)?

TABLE 5.1a Questions That Must Be Asked

	Can Afford Not to Address Formally	*Must Address Formally*
Mega/Outcomes		
Macro/Outputs		
Micro/Products		
Processes		
Inputs		
Evaluation		

2. Which of the questions do you believe your educational agency *and* any of your clients do or do not formally and completely address?

TABLE 5.1b Questions That Are Being Asked

	Do Not Address Formally	*Do Address Formally*
Mega/Outcomes		
Macro/Outputs		
Micro/Products		
Processes		
Inputs		
Evaluation		

3. What are the risks for starting at the Mega level? What are the risks for *not* starting at the Mega level?

Discuss with the planning partners the practicality of starting at the Mega level. Also note the risks of assuming that Macro-level results will lead to positive societal (Mega) payoffs and consequences.

In an attempt to stay well within their comfort zones, many planners feel they must restrict themselves to what is attainable. They will assert that we should not be academic, but should only seek that which we believe we can deliver. This type of self-restriction flies in the face of rationality. The old adage, "Your reach should exceed your grasp," encourages us to push the envelope, that is, intend to accomplish more than we otherwise believe possible.

The Strategic Planning Agreement Table (Table 5.2) enables planning partners to understand that if they don't select Mega, they limit their intentions to current understanding and conventional wisdom. They might be reminded that our educational system, by and large but not always, has not been successful in delivering useful results.

B. Measurability of the Ideal Vision

Once an ideal vision has been stated, there should be precise and measurable indicators you can use to plot your pathway—develop your strategic map—and to evaluate your progress as well as your final accomplishments. Everything is measurable, at least on one of the four scales.

Target type of scale for planning elements. For each element of the ideal vision statement, identify if it is measurable on an interval or ratio scale. Because interval and ratio are the more reliable measures, it is best to have as many as possible. Fill in the elements on your own table, then check off the proper category (nominal, ordinal, interval, ratio) for each:

Ideal Vision Element	Nominal	Ordinal	Interval	Ratio
—				
—				
—				
etc.				

TABLE 5.2 A Strategic Planning Agreement Table (based on Kaufman, 1992b, 1995)

| | RESPONSE | | | |
| | Stake-holders | | QM Planners | |
	Y	N	Y	N
1. Each school, as well as the total educational system, will contribute to the learners' and societal current and future success, survival, health, and well-being.				
2. Each school, as well as the total educational system, will contribute to the learners' and societal current and future quality of life.				
3. Learners' and societal current and future survival, health, and well-being will be part of the system's and each of its schools' mission objectives.				
4. Each educational function will have objectives which contribute to #1, #2, and #3.				
5. Each job/task/activity/project will have objectives which contribute to #1, #2, #3, and #4.				
6. A Needs Assessment will identify and document any gaps in results at the operational levels of #1, #2, #3, #4, and #5.				
7. Educational learning requirements will be generated from the Needs identified and selected based on the results of #6.				
8. The results of #6 may recommend noneducational intervention(s).				
9. Evaluation and continuous improvement will use data from comparing results with objectives for #1, #2, #3, #4, and #5.				

51

Scoring: Add up the number of elements in each of the measurement types. Then calculate the percentages of each type. The more reliable the measures and criteria for each element of the ideal vision, the greater confidence we may have in them. Interval and ratio indicators provide the best basis for determining whether or not we have achieved our objectives (in fact, we define an "objective" as a result measurable on an interval or ratio scale). They provide the more solid basis for evaluation and continuous improvement.

A score over 35 shows you are in the right area; a score of 50 is the most desirable. A score of 20 should encourage you to make all of your elements measurable on an interval or ratio scale. By limiting yourself to nominal or ordinal indicators (indicated by a score of minus 25), you risk confusion concerning what to achieve and when you have achieved the results you intended to deliver.

Revision recommendations: For each indicator in the nominal or ordinal scale, ask: "How will I know when this has been accomplished?" Imagine having to go to court next week in order to prove to the judge that you have delivered what you promised (accountability for results). Often the unchallenged belief that something is not measurable (or you are dehumanized if you do measure it) unthinkingly wins the day. But if you can name it, you know that it exists. Push for more reliability of measurement as you move from nominal and ordinal to interval and ratio.

Make sure your objectives are useful. For each element in the ideal vision, and also for the entire ideal vision, use the algorithm in Figure 2.1. As you revise your ideal vision—or create one—keep the following in mind:

1. Remember that an ideal vision *is* ideal. It defines, in measurable performance terms, the kind of world you and your partners want for tomorrow's child.
2. Take the long view.
3. Dream. Be idealistic. Imagine a perfect world.
4. Don't worry if your vision doesn't seem achievable at first. It might not be realized in your lifetime or during your children's, but at least you will know where you are headed. Furthermore, you can track your continuous progress.

5. Take heart that you and your organization are not responsible for achieving all of the ideal vision, just a part of it.

6. Define ends, not means (or resources). Make the ends, or objectives, measurable on an interval or ratio scale. This is not the place for poetry but for measurable indicators of the kind of world you want for your grandchildren.

7. In writing objectives, including the ideal vision, use the "ABCD"s below, following the process for writing objectives (see Table 2.1, p. 11):

A(udience): Recipients, target groups. Who benefits?

B(ehavior): Performance, accomplishment, result. These are ends, not means.

C(onditions): Under what circumstances and environment will the performance or behavior be accomplished?

D(ata): Criteria, ideally on an interval or ratio scale, that will be used to calibrate success. This indicates how you can tell when you have reached your desired ends.

Now, derive your own version of an ideal vision with the help of Table 5.3. Or, use a general ideal vision and have your planning partners select what to keep, delete, or modify.

C. Level and Scope of Strategic Planning

What level of primary focus did you select for the strategic plan?

1. Mega/societal
2. Macro/organizational
3. Micro/individual or small group
4. Processes, methods, activities, interventions
5. Resources, inputs

Analyzing your present level. Using Table 5.4, take the mission statement (or, better, the mission objective you derived for your strategic plan) and determine which elements deal with Mega, Macro, Micro (or, inappropriately, with means and/or resources).

TABLE 5.3 Deriving an Ideal Vision

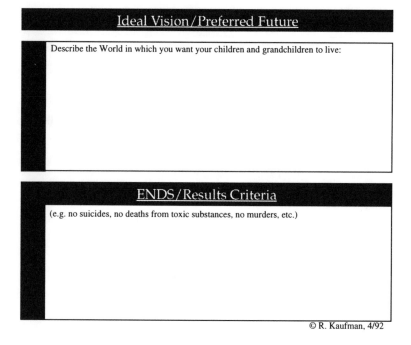

Ideal Vision/Preferred Future

Describe the World in which you want your children and grandchildren to live:

ENDS/Results Criteria

(e.g. no suicides, no deaths from toxic substances, no murders, etc.)

© R. Kaufman, 4/92

TABLE 5.4 Determining If Your Mission or Ideal Vision Is Appropriate

Mission Elements:	Target		Ends Level		
	Means	Ends	Mega	Macro	Micro
a)					
b)					
c) etc...					

NOTE: Step 1: List each element of the mission. Step 2: For each, determine if it relates to a means or an end. Step 3: If an element relates to an end, determine whether it is focused at the Micro, Macro, or Mega level. Step 4: If an element relates to a means, ask: "What result would I get if I got or accomplished this?" Keep asking the same question until an end is identified.

Determining the level. Analyze the plan and its mission objective—"Where are you headed?" *and* "What criteria (on an interval or ratio scale) will be used to measure success?" Remember that a mission statement only identifies where you are headed. Pay close attention to the performance indicators, or criteria, used. Identify who really is to be the primary client and beneficiary of what the plan will deliver.

When the primary client and beneficiary of the strategic plan is the society or the community (as identified in the ideal vision), and when there are performance indicators included in the mission objective that identify such (no murders; all graduates and completers employed at or above subsistence level for at least 6 months), the plan is Mega-level referenced. When the mission objective and performance indicators are targeted at organizational contributions alone (such as having 92% levels of graduates, completers, or merit scholars—perhaps without *also* requiring they be successful beyond graduation), and the indicators are *not* linked to selected elements in the ideal vision, the plan is at the Macro level. When the mission objective and performance indicators intend to achieve results for individuals or small groups (learner grades, scores on the SAT, Latin Club members), the plan is at the Micro level.

When the plan addresses methods and means (contact hours, time on computers, hours committed to writing), it is process related. If it focuses on resources (number of computers, number of learners per classroom, teacher credential levels, class size), the plan is input/resources related.

Scoring: Record your score on the form in Appendix A. If your selected scope is all Mega—it relates and will contribute to the achievement of the ideal vision—give yourself 100 points. If your selected scope is some Mega with mostly Macro, give yourself 70 points. If your scope is Micro, give yourself 20 points. If your scope is processes and/or resources, deduct 100 points.

Revision recommendations: Note that as you continue throughout this section, you are advised to consistently move all planning activities into the Mega level. To the extent that your planning remains results oriented and keeps the ideal vision in mind, you can attain maximum scores.

The scales used here are based upon experiential judgments and should not be interpreted as being more than ordinal scale estimates of value. If your score is 100, you have developed a practically focused strategic plan. If you score 70 or above, you are in satisfactory condition and can benefit from shifting all of your objectives to achievement of Mega-level results. If you score 20 points, you are, like most educational agencies, more concerned with courses than you are with what learners are able to do—within school and as they become contributing citizens. The score of 20 indicates that you are results focused, but still with some of the basics of a strategic planning approach that will let you move to Mega. If you have a negative 100, you might think about taking up politics.

Getting to Mega. Re-select the scope to be Mega, and then link the balance of the strategic plan (Macro/Micro, process/resources) to that. In order to get the strategic planning partners and stakeholders to reconcile and commit to the Mega level, use Table 5.2.

Be certain to have each major stakeholder respond and sign or initial each of the elements. If any person demurs from a "yes" response, ask this individual to write down exactly, in measurable terms, what he or she has in mind.

In order to move from the starting reference (usually a mixture of means—inputs, processes—with Micro-level, plus a few Macro-level, objectives), follow the guidance in Figure 2.2 (p. 9). For each lower-than-Mega element ask: "If I accomplish this, what result would we get?"

Keep asking this until there is a statement of Mega-level-related results. Identify elements of the ideal vision that you have selected to form your mission objective. Make certain that each ideal vision element selected is represented in your mission objective.

Making statements measurable. Often planning partners demur that there are just some things that are not measurable. Note the old adage, "If you can name it, you can measure it." Even by saying that some things are not measurable, they are making two piles: *measurable things* and *nonmeasurable things*. Doing this is actually making a measurement. Naming, albeit the least reliable level of measurement, is measurement all the same (known as the nomi-

TABLE 5.5 Measurement Scales (from Stevens, 1946, 1951; see also A Taxonomy of Results, Kaufman, 1988, 1992c 1995)

Scale of Measurement	Type of Result
Nominal	Names, labels
Ordinal	Ranks
Interval	Equal scale distances with arbitrary zero point
Ratio	Equal scale distances with known zero point

nal scale). Share with your planning partners the Measurement Scales shown in Table 5.5.

To help people prepare measurable statements—objectives—ask them to use the "Hey Mommy Test." When preparing a statement of results, subject it to the scenario of a child coming to one's mother and saying, "Hey mommy, let me show you how I can (and fill in the would-be objective)." If the objective targets a result, it will be obvious.

For example, how does this sound? "Hey mommy, let me show you that I have a deep and profound love of learning." Without any performance specifications, this doesn't make much sense, does it? Now try this: "Hey mommy, let me show you that I have a deep and profound love of learning by the number of library books I have read and reported on in the last month, the number of other children I have tutored so that they passed their quizzes, and the number of problems I have already solved for next month's exercises." See?

In addition, make certain that all Mega-level objectives (as well as the Macro and Micro ones) pass the "ABCD test" as shown in Table 2.1 (p. 11).

Or use the Mager-type objective format. Figure 5.1 provides a series of templates, or guidelines, to assure your performance indicators do the following:

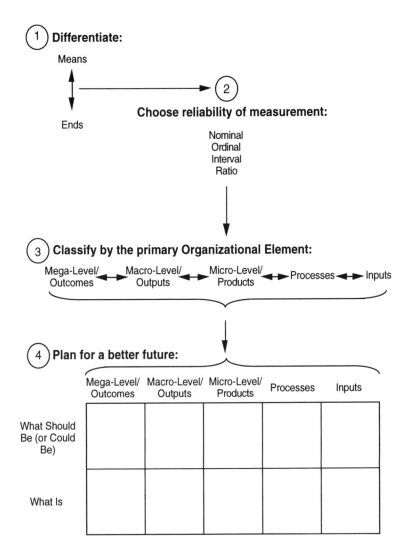

Figure 5.1. Four Templates for Assuring Your Objectives Are Useful (from Kaufman, Grisé, and Watters, 1992)

- Address ends, not means
- Are measurable in rigorous terms (so there is no confusion over whether or not we delivered)
- Address important organizational issues
- Consider both current results and desired ones

Using the order presented in Figure 5.1, let's step through the rationale for each template.

Template 1: **Ends/means.** The first template asks us to assure that our indicators target ends (results, payoffs, consequences, performance) not means (training, teaching, developing).

Template 2: **Reliability of measurement.** The four scales of measurement as shown in Table 5.5:

- Naming (nominal)
- Rank ordering (ordinal)
- Relative scaling with equal scale distances plus an arbitrary zero point like that used for reporting the outside temperature or for standard deviations on tests (interval)
- Absolute scaling with equal scale distances, where there are equal scale distances and a known, fixed zero point as for temperature in Kelvin, weight, and distance (ratio)

When we write useful indicators, the more reliable the criteria, the more confidence we may have in what they target and what we will deliver. Assure that as many of your indicators as possible are measurable on an interval or ratio scale.

Template 3: **Level of organizational result.** Our indicator may target a result at the job or task level (Micro), at the organizational contributions level (Macro), and at the client and societal payoff level (Mega). After working through Templates 1 and 2 above, we can assure that our indicator homes in on an organizational *result* and not on a resource or means (thus also serving as an additional check on Template 1). Using Template 3, we check to assure that we are focused on a result at one of the three levels of planning—Mega, Macro, Micro—and not on resources or methods and means.

Template 4: **Improvement or maintenance.** This is an optional template that allows us to decide if our indicator is focused on maintaining current purposes or if it also bases itself on needs—gaps between current results and desired ones. As we did with Template 3, we determine which level of result—Mega, Macro, or Micro—our indicators primarily address, and we then determine if this result is based on a gap between "what is" and "what should be."

Using these templates can help you know if your performance indicators are correctly formatted and precise. You will also learn if they address important organizational concerns and possible needs.

D. The Planning Partnership

Drucker (1973) gives good advice about "transfer of ownership"—planning so the result is owned by all of the partners. A strategic plan is best when all of the key players (or their creditable representatives) are involved in the development of the plan. In fact, the more involvement (adjusting for the "mob violence" factor—don't get crowds, but true partners), the more the plan will be owned when completed. Identify who is (or will be) involved in the development of the plan, and check against the criteria presented in this audit.

Scoring: Use the Scoring Table to determine your score. The best score is 60. If you get a 10, then get more commitment, participation, and buy-in from your educational partners. If you get a negative score, revise your approach and your plan immediately.

Revision recommendations: If your score was below 60, meet with the current planning partners and ask, "Why have we excluded other partners?" If the answers relate to means ("Not enough time," "They don't know about education," "They have hidden agendas"), review the consequences of not achieving transfer of ownership (see Drucker, 1973).

Identify a stratified random sample of partners. The strata should include those whom the educational agency serves. Usually included are business, government, parents, learners, and educators (see also Kaufman, 1995; Kaufman & Herman, 1991). Seek the agreement for representatives of each group to serve, and get a commitment concerning the time and place they will help plan. However, do not use others as "rubber stamps" because that will backfire. Make certain that they know the ground rules of Mega-level planning, perhaps using the Strategic Planning Agreement (Table 5.2) to assure alignment.

E. Aligning Beliefs and Values

Beliefs and values are the opinions people hold about their world. They may be valid and justifiable or they could be biases and prejudices. Typically, beliefs and values relate to means—inputs or processes (computers teach better than instructors; natives of the nation of Clandestine are not very bright and they like bright colors).

People's perceptions are reality for them, and this soft data should be a part, but not the whole, of developing any strategic plan. When developing the ideal vision, people's beliefs and values should be considered in, but not the focus of, deriving the ideal vision. If the identification of beliefs and values begins the planning process, and/or it is a separate function after the derivation of the ideal vision, people have the opportunity to "regress" to unchallenged assumptions about their world. This separate focus on beliefs and values can be destructive to the development of a useful and shared strategic plan and thus should be avoided. From the existing plan, identify if there is a formal and independent identification of beliefs and values, rather than their being an integrated part of the ideal vision.

Scoring: Use the Scoring Table in Appendix A to determine your points. Beliefs and values certainly exist, and they are important. They usually relate to means and resources and not to objectives (results measurable on an interval or ratio scale). Thus they are not useful as the bases for prescribing destinations. Beliefs and values are inputs to any educational planning and doing activity. They are changeable (Have *you* changed a basic belief or value in the past 10 years?) and, as such, are not a stable basis for developing a strategic plan.

Beliefs and values are best considered only when developing the ideal vision. By invoking them only at that time, we are more free of inserting a bias about "how" we should do education before we have defined "what" it should accomplish—the ideal vision. Doing so will earn you a 100. If you start with beliefs and values, then you will earn a negative score.

Beliefs and values should align with the ideal vision and the educational mission. It is best not to formally review them separately simply because when they are treated outside of the context of an ideal vision, they cannot be objectively considered.

Revision recommendations: Redevelop an ideal vision with beliefs and values data coming into play only as part of the process of identifying the kind of world we want for tomorrow's child. Be certain that the strategic planning process also includes the use of actual performance and impact data.

When a belief or value surfaces, ask "What would be the result and impact if we used this to drive our educational system?" and "What element of the ideal vision does this represent?" Refocus beliefs and values in terms of the ideal vision, and thereby align them with the shared destination for the system.

F. Needs Assessment and Identification

A vital element in strategic planning is a needs assessment, which depends on valid and useful data to identify what is working and what is not. Unfortunately, there is much confusion over what a needs assessment is and what it should include. Here is a special audit you may use to determine if the scope and breadth of your needs assessment is appropriate. This pragmatic tool identifies the essential elements for a useful needs assessment and provides the criteria to identify what might be missing from the current process.

What are needs assessments? What results are we now getting and how do those compare with those we should deliver? Needs assessments provide a process for defining the gaps between current and desired results and providing the justification for identifying and choosing the ways to close those gaps. Before selecting any intervention (be it inservice training, silent prayer, restructuring, or total quality management), conduct a needs assessment to provide the basic data for assuring that solutions, once selected, will deliver desired results.

The literature about needs assessment is confusing and usually contradictory (Witkin, 1994). Some needs assessments deal with ends—gaps in results—whereas others take a more casual approach, dealing with anything people think it is important to have (diversity, more resources, computers). We urge (even plead) that you use a limited definition of need, one that will save you from confusing needs and wants, means and ends.

Another dimension to needs assessment is assuring that needs identified and met at the operational levels (Micro) of an organization will contribute to quality results delivered to external clients (Macro). Not only should we deliver quality to the educational clients, but also help assure that the client is well served, that what we deliver contributes to client satisfaction and contributes to a safe, clean, and healthy shared world (Mega). After all, we can make a client happy with what we deliver (cigarettes, assault weapons) and not do them or our society much good. Linking needs at each level of educational organizational results—Mega, Macro, and Micro—can be critical if your needs assessment is to be both precise and useful.

This portion of the strategic planning audit relates to needs assessment, taking a pragmatic approach. To help keep all of the considerations in mind, Figure 5.2 is a job aid, an algorithm, for assuring that your needs are needs and that they link to the three levels of results and consequences.

Needs—gaps between current results and desired ones—are often confused with wants. A critical success factor is that your plan be based upon ends as well as gaps between current ends and desired ones. Check your strategic plan to see if it defines and identifies needs as gaps in results, not lack of resources and/or inputs. Obtain any statement of needs of your strategic plan, and check against the following criteria. Use the algorithm in Figure 5.3 to assist you in identifying those "need" statements that are ends-related.

A needs assessment-specific audit. As part of your strategic planning audit, this section specifically targets the needs assessment functions. Use the following as a checklist. You can rate each item on a "yes" or "no" basis using the criteria on pp. 66-67 for your judgment.

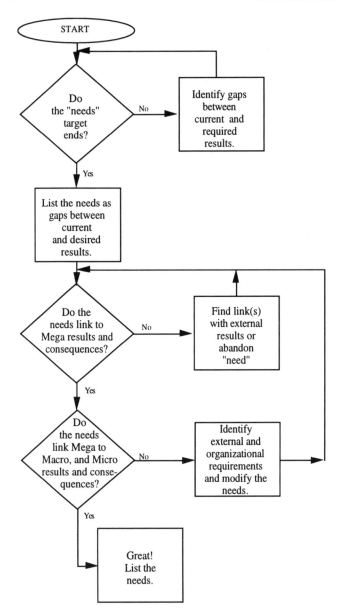

Figure 5.2. A Needs Assessment Job Aid (based on Kaufman, Grisé, and Watters, 1992)

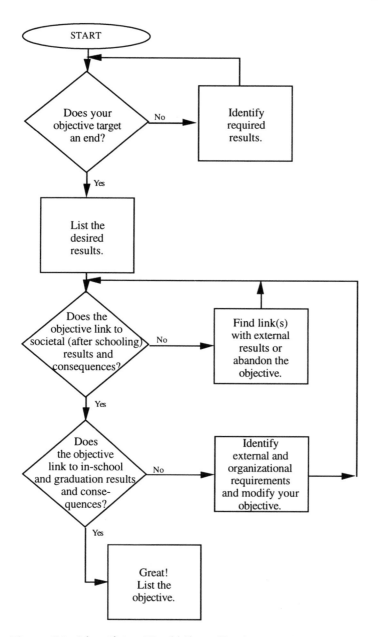

Figure 5.3. Identifying Needs (from Kaufman, 1992c, 1995; with permission)

Criteria		
Elements	Yes	No
1. Needs are identified as gaps between current results and desired results (the gap in results between "what is" and "what should be").		
2. There is a clear distinction made between ends (results, consequences, payoffs) and means (resources, methods, how-to-do-its).		
3. There are three levels of results identified— individual performance (Micro level), organizational contributions (Macro level), and societal and client contributions (Mega level).		
4. The three levels of results include the Mega level (results, payoffs, consequences) for external (outside of the organization) clients.		
5. Mega-level results are clearly related to an ideal vision for both the organization and society that the organization intends to serve.		
6. The three levels of results include the Macro level (results, payoffs, consequences) for the organization itself (not only are there three levels but one of them *is* the Macro level).		
7. The Macro-level results are clearly related to required results at the Mega and ideal vision levels—Macro results are "nested" within the ideal vision and the Mega-level results and payoffs.		
8. The three levels of results include the Micro level (results, payoffs, consequences) for individuals and/or small groups within the organization.		
9. The Micro level results are clearly related to (and nested within) required results at the ideal vision, Mega, and Macro levels of results.		

Criteria		
Elements	*Yes*	*No*
10. Any statement of need is free from any indication of how the need will be met (training, computers, technology).		
11. Any statement of need is free from any indication of what resources will be used to meet the need (personnel, time, money, equipment).		
12. Needs are prioritized on the basis of what it costs to meet the need versus what it will cost to ignore it.		
13. Needs are listed in priority order.		
14. Interventions are selected on the basis of a costs-consequences analysis for each need, or cluster of related needs.		
15. Evaluation criteria are taken directly from the "what should be" dimension of the selected needs.		
16. Evaluation results report the extent to which needs, or families of related needs, have been reduced or eliminated.		

Scoring: The highest rating, a needs assessment's most powerful application, is a "yes" for each of the 16 items. This is rare, however, because conventional wisdom steers people toward a more comfortable "training needs assessment," actually a "training requirements analysis" or, unfortunately, a "solutions/wish list" approach.

Fortunately, what is suggested in other various published approaches, formats, and commercial materials will fail you simply because it encourages you, often incorrectly, to choose and to assume comfortable solutions to problems and opportunities.

Here is a way of rating your needs assessment process in order to discover the importance of the individual characteristics.

1. Absolutely vital elements (that you should probably not go ahead without):
   Element numbers 1, 2, 10, 11, 12, and 13.
2. Elements that are essential for total organizational success (if you want the entire organization to be responsive and responsible) include:
   Element numbers 1, 2, 3, 4, 5, 6, 7, 8, 9, 10, 11, 12, 13, and 14.
3. If you are only interested in an organization's success in the short run, then include only these elements:
   Element numbers 1, 2, 6, 8, 9, 10, 11, 12, and 13.
4. If you are only interested in making Micro-level changes for the performance of individuals or small groups, then simply include:
   Element numbers 1, 2, 8, 9, 10, 11, 12, and 13.
5. If you are also interested in the usefulness of your needs assessment in assisting you and your organization in continuous improvement, then add these:
   Element numbers 14, 15, and 16.

Other needs assessment approaches. A way to classify and determine the suitability of any needs assessment approach, process, or model is to compare it with the criteria in this audit. Many existing approaches to needs assessment fall outside of the elements listed here because they focus primarily on means and resources, or only attend to perceptions of needs.

The Mega level of concern for needs assessment is part of a new organizational paradigm. Societal concern and payoffs are vital for organizational survival and success. If your organization does not intend for everything it uses, does, and delivers to be useful to both the client and our shared society, it will predictably fail. Aligning what organizations use, do, and deliver with the payoffs for clients and society is fundamental. This needs assessment audit will allow you to identify the extent to which your process will be practical and appropriate for today's organizational realities and imperatives.

Scoring: Refer to the Scoring Table in Appendix A. In the first part of this short-form audit, a score of 50 lets you know you are on target and not confusing ends with means. A score of 10 shows that you are on your way but risk including some premature solutions by calling means ends. A minus score shows that the conventional—and dangerous—wisdom about needs as being wants and methods/resources has likely headed you in a nonuseful (and perhaps even dangerous) direction.

In the second part of this short form, an added 40 points shows you are developing a useful strategic plan based on important—Mega-level—needs. An added 25 points shows you are limiting your needs assessment reach to the educational organization. Likewise, an additional 10 points shows you are operating at the course level and might be shortchanging yourself, your learners, your partners, and your community.

Revision recommendations: Collect all statements of needs. Convert those that deal with inputs and processes into ends-related statements by asking, for each one: "If I accomplished or obtained this, what would be the result?" Keep asking this question as you push each from inputs to processes to products to outputs, and finally to outcomes. As you identify needs, summarize them in an orderly and objective manner.

Here is a sample needs assessment summary format (customize it to match your educational organizational realities) of possible need areas. Table 5.6 does the following: (1) summarizes needs at three levels of results (Mega, Macro, and Micro); (2) allows entries for means and resources (called quasi-needs) so they are not confused with needs (gaps in results), and (3) provides the opportunity to consider both results and consequences for several sources of possible needs.

The Organizational Elements Model (OEM). Sort your existing needs into the OEM (Table 2.3, p. 20) and identify the following:

1. Empty cells
2. Cells that are full

TABLE 5.6 A Basic Needs Assessment Summary Format (based on Kaufman, Grisé, & Watters, 1992)

Current Results	Possible Means	Required Results	Related Ideal Vision Element	Need Level		
				Mega	Macro	Micro

3. Rational linkages between the elements (Do the "what should be" processes derive rationally from the outcomes, outputs, and products?)

4. Empty cells and/or relationships that are not sensible among the elements

For each "need" apply the algorithm in Figure 5.4. Revise as required.

G. Identifying the Current Mission

Most organizations and strategic plans have a mission statement, but few have mission objectives. And still fewer have mission objectives free of statements of means and resources. This audit phase lets you review your existing mission. Is it precise and comprehensive? Check your plan's mission against these criteria.

Scoring: Turn to the Scoring Table to determine your results. A mission objective, as all other objectives, must state in no uncertain terms "where we are headed," and "how we will know when we have arrived." This important principle was earlier identified as Critical Success Factor 4 and also as a variation of Critical Success Factor 2.

If you scored 40 points, you are right on target. If you scored 15, you are results oriented but lacking the precision and rigor required for strategic planning (that which defines useful destinations and allows you to decide how to get the required building-block results). If your plan earned a negative score, your planning is stuck in a process/solutions mode that does not serve you well. An additional 40 points shows you are really on target (Mega oriented), whereas only 20 points shows you are limiting yourself to courses and performance tests and not working with the big picture.

Revision recommendations: Convert each process and/or resource into an end-statement. For each, ask: "If I accomplished or obtained this, what would be the result?" Keep asking that question as you push each one from inputs/processes to products to outputs, and finally to outcomes. Apply the algorithm in Figure 2.1 (p. 6) and revise as required. Also, apply the measurability of objectives aids identified (use the "ABCD" and the Mager-type reference here).

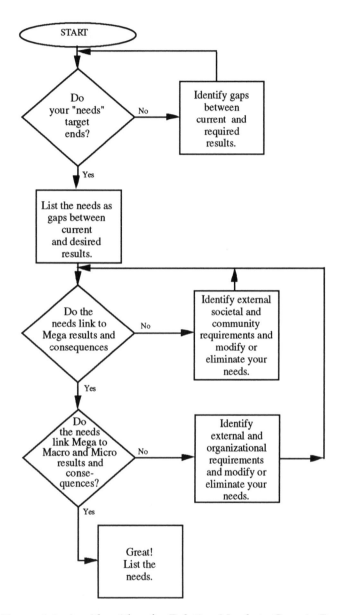

Figure 5.4. An Algorithm for Relating Needs to Gaps in Results and Assuring That Results Link at All Three Levels

5.2 Planning

A. Identifying Strengths, Weaknesses, Opportunities, and Threats (SWOTs)

Make certain your calibrations are objective. The success of a strategic plan may depend upon identifying the strengths, weaknesses, opportunities, and threats. Based upon the mission objectives that plot a continuous improvement pathway toward the ideal vision, the SWOTs must be objective calibrations of reality.

Scoring: Turn to the Scoring Table to assess your SWOTs analysis. Check for the "reality" that so many planners want and should have—at the right time in the planning process. Done at this stage in strategic planning, it is realistic. If you received 95 points, you have an excellent SWOT analysis, at the right time and place. If you earned 10-25 points you should rethink where and when you do your SWOT analysis. Any negative points suggest you are not considering important aspects in assuring the validity and usefulness of your strategic plan.

Revision recommendations: Determine SWOTs, supporting them by data. Remind the planning partners of the obligation to develop a strategic plan that will deliver measurably useful education.

Determine matches and mismatches. If an appropriate SWOT analysis were accomplished, there would be both hard data (performance grounded: the needs assessment) and soft data (perceptions: the ideal vision; existing mission). Check to see if the data all agree. This step compares the data to detect agreements and disagreements.

The analysis: Assure that both the hard and soft data are results related. Identify that each targets ends and not means. Also, determine the extent to which the selected level for planning (Mega, Macro, Micro) have been maintained. Finally, match those hard and soft data indicators that agree as well as those where there are differences.

Scoring: Use the Scoring Table. A score of 70 indicates that you have realized that people's perceptions are reality for them and thus are important. You also collected and used hard performance data to assure that you are getting an appropriate balance between actual performance and perceived performance. A score of 45 indicates you are heading in the right direction for balance and should increase the use of hard data. A negative score indicates you are operating on perceptions alone, which could lead to a strategic plan that will disappoint you and your partners.

Revision recommendations: Re-collect data, obtaining the missing elements. Explain, again, to the planning partners that accountability is ultimately for results. Although it is tempting to "please" people (the political option), the basic responsibility for an education system is to prepare learners to be self-sufficient, self-reliant good neighbors.

Reconcile differences. It is vital that the strategic plan be understood and acceptable to all stakeholders. Differences must be reconciled on the basis of meeting the mission objective—thus moving continuously closer to the ideal vision—and the needs, not on keeping the peace. Differences are best resolved by comparing the differences with the ideal vision and the mission objective. Determine the processes used to reconcile differences, and rate the strategic plan and process.

Scoring: Enter the values for your difference resolution in the Scoring Table. If you earned 175 points, your strategic plan will likely be successful in enrolling all key players in its nature and purpose. Under 100 points, without negative points, shows you could benefit from a larger representation in doing the strategic plan. A negative score shows that a paradigm shift in strategic planning has not yet occurred.

Revision recommendations: Convene the planning group; then, use the ideal vision and the mission objective. Compare each difference with these statements, asking the group to resolve differences. Review with them the Basic Questions in Table 3.1 (p. 29) and the Strategic Planning Agreement (Table 5.2, p. 51), along with your partnership involvement as required. This might require redoing part of the strategic plan, especially the scoping and planning sections.

B. Selecting Long- and Short-Term Missions

Based on the above data and agreements, the long-term (year 2010, 2000, 1998) missions and shorter term missions (next year, this year) should be stated. All missions should represent continuous improvement toward the ideal vision.

Scoring: Obtain the resulting mission objectives and determine your score. With a score of 175 points, you are doing an excellent job in this part of the strategic plan. With a score of 50 points, you should extend the reach of the plan to include further-out dates and the ideal vision. A negative score indicates that old paradigms are still operating, and your strategic plan is dealing more with tactics and means than with strategies.

Revision recommendations: Prepare mission objectives for distant and close-in results. Make certain they deal with ends and not means or resources. Use the ideal vision and assure that the objectives describe the measurable path from current results to reach the mission objective and the ideal vision. Apply the algorithms for objectives used earlier.

C. Deriving Decision Rules (Policies)

Having policies in place that can be used to make decisions is useful as a guide once one moves from planning to implementation. Policies that are related to the ideal vision, mission objectives, and needs will allow anyone in the system to make decisions that contribute. Obtain the strategic plan, and identify the decision rules. Score as follows using the Scoring Table.

Scoring: A zero or negative score indicates your strategic planning effort can be helped by deriving decision rules. A positive score, of course, shows that you are doing a thorough, efficient, and effective strategic planning activity.

Revision recommendations: Simple. Develop and obtain approval for decision rules that relate directly to the results required by the vision and mission objectives.

D. Developing Your Strategic Plan

Any plan must be put to work, be used, and deliver continuous improvement toward the ideal vision. Analyze the strategic plan and determine your score.

E. Implementation and Continuous Improvement

While this next phase of being strategic is not strictly strategic planning, nevertheless, it is where everything that has been planned will come to life—the application. If a strategic plan does not translate into useful education, then all has been a waste of time and effort.

In this phase, the following must be accomplished:

1. Identify and select ways and means to accomplish the objectives and lead ever closer to the ideal vision. This step includes costs-consequences analyses.
2. Manage implementation.
3. Determine met and unmet objectives—based on the needs met, and those still unmet—and revise and continuously improve as required.

Scoring: Use the audit items in the Scoring Table to help you check your implementation for what was strategically planned. If you scored 100, your linking of interventions to your strategic plan is excellent. If you scored between 40 and 80, you are on the right road but could benefit from formalizing your intervention selection. If you earned a negative score, you should formally link your how-to-do-its to the strategic plan.

Revision recommendations: A checklist may be used that asks each educator and educational team to identify

1. The measurable objective to which your current or intended intervention (courses, course elements, programs, projects, activities) is targeted
2. The measurable criteria from which targeted measurable objectives will be used to provide evaluation and continuous improvement
3. The element of the primary mission objective that successful completion of the intervention will contribute
4. The element of the ideal vision that successful completion of the intervention will contribute

F. Determining Met/Unmet Objectives

It is not enough to have good intentions; it is also vital to carry through to successful completion: the delivery of learners who are successful during education and later as citizens. This audit is about neither implementation nor management, but there are some elements against which you may calibrate your management.

Scoring: Use the Scoring Table to rate your management.

Revision recommendations: Review the principles of management and executive performance as well as quality management and quality management plus (e.g., Kaufman & Zahn, 1993) and review newer works in management (e.g., Argyris, 1991; Barker, 1989, 1992, 1993; Block, 1993; Branson, 1988; Conner, 1992; Kaufman, 1992, 1995; Kaufman and Herman, 1991; Roberts, 1987; Rummler and Brache, 1990; and Senge, 1990).

There are new and better ways of managing the educational enterprise. You and your educational partners can help yourselves and your associates by adopting some of these ideas. The principles and understandings of quality management are very important, especially if the substance and not just the compliance aspects are used. Continuous improvement, based upon needs, can be vital for your organization.

Summary

This audit will allow you to calibrate how useful—yes, and *successful*—your strategic plan will be. Apply this process sensibly, intending only to use the results for improving, not for blaming.

Appendix A

Scoring Table

Topic	Your Response	Score	Grade	Your Score
Depth of the Ideal Vision (p. 47)	Ideal/Mega	100	A	
	Macro	30	B	
	Micro	20	D	
	Processes	–30	F	
	Inputs/resources	–40	F	
	"Attainable/practical" Mega	10	B	
	"Attainable/practical" Macro	5	C	
	"Attainable/practical" Micro	2	D	
	"Attainable/practical" Process	–35	F	
	"Attainable/practical" Resources	–45	F	
	No vision statement used	–75	F	
Ideal Vision Prepared for the Societal Level? (p. 48)	Ideal vision describes in measurable performance terms the kind of world we want for tomorrow's child	50	A	
	Ideal vision identifies future societal conditions but does not include measurable criteria	20	C	
	Ideal vision describes the kind of educational organization desired	20	C	
	Ideal vision is about resources and processes that are desired for the educational agency	–25	F	

Topic	Your Response	Score	Grade	Your Score
Measurability of the Ideal Vision (p. 50)	90–100% of elements are on interval and/or ratio scale	50	A	
	60–89% are interval and/or ratio	35	B	
	40–59% are interval and/or ratio	20	C	
	Below 40% interval and/or ratio	–25	F	
Level/Scope of Strategic Planning (p. 53)	Mega	100	A	
	Some Mega with mostly Macro	70	B	
	Micro	20	D	
	Processes and/or resources	–100	F	
The Planning Partnership (p. 59)	A representative group, from all major stakeholders (parents, educators, employers, learners, minorities, etc.) in your educational programs who have developed and recommended the strategic plan	20	A	
	Planning team was from the central office and the school board, with a few teachers and a student or two	10	C	
	Plan done by the central office and approved by the Board	–25	F	
[BONUS]	Plan is understood and actively supported by educators, parents, and the community	*40		
Aligning Beliefs & Values (p. 61)	Beliefs and values formally obtained and used as the starting place for the strategic planning	–100	F	

Topic	Your Response	Score	Grade	Your Score
	No formal collection of beliefs and values, but rather discussing them is a part of deriving the ideal vision	100	A	
	Beliefs and values are ignored—even when developing the ideal vision	–100	F	
Needs Assessment and Identification (p. 62)	Clear distinctions made between means and ends	50	A	
	Most choices are ends but a few are means disguised as ends	10	D	
	Much confusion over what are means and what are ends	0 or less	F	
	Plans being developed using Mega-level needs	40	A	
	Plans being developed with consideration for the educational organization only (Macro level)	25	B	
	Plans being developed for a singluar course or at student-skills level only	10	D	
Identifying the Current Mission (p. 71)	Mission includes measurable criteria, stating both "where we are headed" and "how we can tell when we have arrived"	40	A	
	Mission only states intentions of a destination ("excellence in education," "a place where everyone can learn," etc.)	15	C	
	Mission only identifies process and resources ("individualized learning opportunities," "caring teaching and a safe environment," etc.)	–40	F	

Topic	Your Response	Score	Grade	Your Score
[BONUS]	Mission targets—and contributes to—results at the Mega and Macro levels	*40		
Identifying SWOTs (p. 73)	SWOTs were determined	25	B	
	SWOTs were determined at the stage of strategic planning after the ideal vision, the missions, and the needs were identified— not at the outset of strategic planning	25	A	
	SWOTs are supported by performance data	45	A	
	SWOTs were identified but don't seem to be supported by performance data	10	D	
	No SWOTs analysis	–50	F	
Determining Matches and Mismatches (p. 73)	Both hard and soft data have been identified for key variables	70	A	
	Some hard data has been collected, but most data are soft	45	C	
	Only soft (perception) data have been collected	–50	F	
Reconciling Differences (p. 74)	All differences were resolved by the planning team and/or representatives of the key stakeholders	100	A	
	Differences were resolved by negotiations with small stakeholder groups on issues that concerned them	20	C	
	Planning staff unilaterally resolved differences	–50	F	
	The ideal vision and the mission objective were used in resolving differences	75	A	

Topic	Your Response	Score	Grade	Your Score
	Reconciliation was done without relating to the ideal vision or mission	-25	F	
	Reconciliations were often made in order to placate one or more groups	-50	F	
Selecting Long- and Short-Term Missions (p. 74)	Clear objectives for distant and near results to be delivered have been identified	100	A	
	Only near objectives (1–3 years) have been identified	50	B	
	No mission objectives have been derived	-75	F	
	Objectives are means and resources related	-75	F	
[BONUS]	Objectives identify required measurable progress toward the ideal vision	*75		
Deriving Decision Rules (p. 75)	Decision rules (policies) exist that relate directly to the ideal vision and mission objectives	50	A	
	Decision rules (policies) exist, but they mostly relate to resources and process	0	D	
	No decision rules (policies) are stated	-25	F	
Developing Your Strategic Plan (p. 75)	The strategic plan identifies en route objectives that will likely deliver continuous improvement	100	A	
	The strategic plan identifies ways and means—resources and methods—to achieve the objectives and move continuously toward the ideal vision	100	A	

Topic	Your Response	Score	Grade	Your Score
	The ways and means selected were derived from a formal costs-consequences analysis	100	A	
	The strategic plan only deals with means and resources	−100	F	
	No formal costs-consequences analysis was performed to select means and resources	−75	F	
	The plan is approved by the planning committee and/or key stakeholders	75	B	
	The plan is used every time a decision is made by staff members and the board	100	A	
	The plan is not used, and has not been since it was generated	−100	F	
	There is continuous evaluation of the plan based on its performance	100	A	
	There have been results-referenced changes made to the strategic plan since its implementation	100	A	
	There have been changes and/or additions to the mission objective for the educational agency as a result of strategic planning and progress toward the ideal vision	100	A	
Implementation/ Continuous Improvement (p. 76)	Every methods-means, program, project, activity, and intervention was formally linked to Mega and Macro objectives	100	A	

Topic	Your Response	Score	Grade	Your Score
	Every methods-means, program, project, activity, and intervention was selected on the basis of a costs-consequences analysis	100	A	
	Every methods-means, program, project, activity, and intervention was informally linked to Mega and Micro objectives	40	C	
	Every methods-means, program, project, activity, and intervention was selected on the basis of an informal costs-consequences analysis	40	C	
	Methods-means, programs, projects, activities and interventions were not formally linked to Mega and Macro objectives	−100	F	
	No estimates of costs-consequences were made for the selected methods-means, programs, projects, activities, or interventions	−100	F	
Determining Met/Unmet Objectives (p. 79)	Each intervention— program, project, activity, course—has measurable objectives	100	A	
	Each intervention tracks its progress toward its objectives in order to identify what is working, what should be changed, what to delete, what to add	100	A	
	The results of evaluation are used for fixing and continuous improvement and never for blaming	100	A	

Topic	Your Response	Score	Grade	Your Score
	Educational teams are used to identify and resolve existing problems	20	C	
	Everyone on the educational teams shares the same process objectives and contributes uniquely to the results	20	D	
	Supervisors closely monitor compliance of educators as they do their work	0	D	
	No formal objectives are set or used	–50	F	
	There are no revisions made to objectives once they are set and approved	–60	F	
	Central office regularly inspects the work of educators	–25	F	
YOUR OVERALL STRATEGIC PLANNING SCORE				

Appendix B

A Calibration of Your Progress

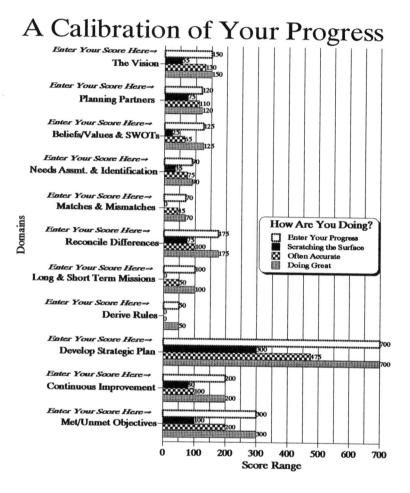

Appendix C

Glossary of Terms

Building-block results. Products that will, when accomplished along with other products (or functions), deliver a larger result.

Comfort zone. The areas (and stimuli) with which one feels nonthreatened; the usual, familiar territory where one's paradigm works well.

Costs-consequences analysis. A "coarse-grained analysis" that identifies the relationship between what is put into an intervention and what comes out; in other words, the relationship between the value/worth of the contributions and the results attained, or the payoff one gets from what is put into the system. It is an alternative to an economic analysis of return-on-investment that takes into consideration more detailed variables of cost and results than most operational educators have time to obtain or data to support.

External scanning. An analysis that identifies strengths, weaknesses, opportunities, and threats arising external to the organization.

Function. A product that will, with other products, lead to a larger result. A function is not a process.

Hard data. Data based on independently verifiable performance.

Ideal vision. The preferred future in terms of the state of the world and conditions and quality of life for you, your organization, and your world; one useful criterion is to describe the world in which you want tomorrow's child to live.

Inputs. The ingredients, or starting conditions, used by the organization.

Internal scanning. An analysis that identifies strengths, weaknesses, opportunities, and threats arising form within the organization.

Interval scale. A scale of measurement that has equal scale distances but has an arbitrary zero point.

Macro-level thinking/planning. Activity where the primary client and beneficiary of what gets planned and delivered is the school or educational system itself.

Mega-level thinking/planning. Activity where the primary client and beneficiary of what gets planned and delivered is the society and community.

Micro-level thinking/planning. Activity where the primary client and beneficiary of what gets planned and delivered is individuals and small groups within the school or system.

Mission objective. The overall statement of what the organization commits to deliver. As with any objective, results are stated through criteria that demonstrate progress being made (or not) toward the meeting of the ideal vision. These results are in interval or ratio scale terms.

Mission statement. Where one is headed—the destination (but not defined in interval or ratio scale terms).

Need. At least for rational planning, the gap between current and desired or required results.

Needs assessment. The process of identifying gaps in results (needs), placing them in priority order, and selecting the most important for reduction or elimination.

Nominal scale. A scale of measurement that simply names something.

Objective. A statement of intended results that includes (a) what results are to be obtained, (b) who or what will display the result, (c) under what conditions the result will be observed, and (d) what criteria (using interval or ratio scale measurement) will be used.

Ordinal scale. A scale of measurement that rank orders two or more things.

Organizational Elements Model (OEM). The elements that make up that which every organization uses (inputs), does (processes), accomplishes (products), delivers (outputs) outside of itself, plus the external consequences of all of it (outcomes) in and for society; results at the Micro level are products; those at the Macro level are outputs; and those at the Mega level are outcomes.

Outcomes. The external—outside the school or system—payoffs and consequences of the inputs, processes, products, and outputs in and for the society and community (Mega-level results).

Outputs. The results that are or could be delivered to society (Macro-level results).

Paradigm. The boundary of a system and the set of ground rules that one uses to operate within that boundary.

Paradigm shift. The situation where old boundaries and associated antique ground rules don't square with reality; they have shifted to a new reality where revised boundaries and ground rules are appropriate.

Primary mission objective. An objective based on the part of the ideal vision the educational agency commits to deliver and to continuously move toward. The primary mission objective serves as the basic direction in which your educational organization will head—the guiding star. It states the macro-level results (outputs) to be delivered.

Problem identification and resolution model (six steps). A framework and steps for (a) identifying problems (based on needs); (b) determining detailed performance requirements and identifying possible methods and means for meeting the requirements; (c) selection of methods and means; (d) implementation; (e) determining effectiveness and efficiency of performance; and an ongoing step, (f) revising as required.

Processes. The methods, means, activities, programs, and "how-to's" used to turn the inputs into accomplishments.

Products. The building-block results accomplished by working with the inputs and using the processes (Micro-level results).

Quasi need/quasi needs assessment. A gap in processes or resources (but not a gap in results) or the collection and prioritizing of gaps in processes or resources; sometimes confused with needs assessment, which causes means, methods, and/or resources to be selected without linking them to gaps in performance.

Ratio scale. A scale of measurement that has equal scale distances and a known zero point.

Soft data. Data based upon individual perceptions that are not independently verifiable.

Strategic planning. A process for defining useful (and possible new and additional) objectives and their linkage to effective and efficient tactics. The model offered here has four phases: scoping, data collecting, planning, and implementation and evaluation; this differs from usual planning approaches that assume current objectives as useful and valid and tend to react to existing problems.

Strategic planning plus (SP+). An approach that extends conventional strategic planning and tactical planning by also identifying the kind of future we want to create for tomorrow's child (Mega-level results) while also taking care of today's housekeeping problems.

Strategic thinking. Knowing what to achieve, being able to justify the direction, and then finding the best ways to get there; being strategic is proactive and differs from being reactive to problems as they surface; strategic thinking is the most important product of strategic planning.

SWOTs. Strengths, weaknesses, opportunities, and threats.

System. The sum total of individual parts, working alone and together, to achieve a common purpose.

System approach to education. Treating the entire educational enterprise as a system where a change in one part causes changes in all other parts; creates a total school system, not a system of schools.

Value added. The extent to which we recover costs and deliver beyond the break-even point for a delivered output, or result.

References and
Suggested Readings

Argyris, C. (1991, May-June). Teaching smart people to learn. *Harvard Business Review.*

Banathy, B. H. (1991). *Systems design of education: A journey to create the future.* Englewood Cliffs, NJ: Educational Technology.

Barker, J. A. (1989). *The business of paradigms: Discovering the future* [Videotape]. Burnsville, MN: ChartHouse Learning.

Barker, J. A. (1992). *Future edge: Discovering the new paradigms of success.* New York: William Morrow.

Barker, J. A. (1993). *Paradigm pioneers: Discovering the future series* [Videotape]. Burnsville, MN: ChartHouse Learning.

Block, P. (1993). *Stewardship.* San Francisco: Berrett-Koehler.

Branson, R. K. (1988). Why schools can't improve: The upper limit hypothesis. *Journal of Instructional Development, 4.*

Conner, D. R. (1992). *Managing at the speed of sound.* New York: Random House-Villard.

Cook, W. J., Jr. (1990). *Bill Cook's strategic planning for America's schools* (Rev. ed.). Birmingham, AL and Arlington, VA: Cambridge Management Group and the American Association of School Administrators.

Deming, W. E. (1982). *Quality, productivity, and competitive position.* Cambridge: MIT, Center for Advanced Engineering Study.

Drucker, P. F. (1973). *Management: Tasks, responsibilities, practices.* New York: Harper & Row.

Drucker, P. F. (1992, September-October). The new society of organizations. *Harvard Business Review*, pp. 95-104.

Drucker, P. F. (1993). *Post-capitalist society.* New York: HarperBusiness.

Hammer, M., & Champy, J. (1993). *Reengineering the corporation: A manifesto for business revolution.* New York: HarperBusiness.

Hammer, M., & Stanton, S. A. (1995). *The reengineering revolution: A handbook.* New York: HarperCollins.

Kanter, R. M. (1989). *When giants learn to dance: Mastering the challenges of strategy, management, and careers in the 1990s.* New York: Simon & Schuster.

Kaufman, R. (1987, October). A needs assessment primer. *Training & Development Journal.*

Kaufman, R. (1988a, July). Needs assessment: A menu. *Performance & Instruction.*

Kaufman, R. (1988b, September). Preparing useful performance indicators. *Training & Development Journal.*

Kaufman, R. (1988c). *Planning educational systems: A results-based approach.* Lancaster, PA: Technomic.

Kaufman, R. (1991, December). Toward total quality "plus." *Training & Development Journal.*

Kaufman, R. (1992a, April). The challenge of total quality management in education. *International Journal of Educational Reform.*

Kaufman, R. (1992b, July). Comfort and change: Natural enemies. *Educational Technology.*

Kaufman, R. (1992c). *Strategic planning plus: An organizational guide.* Newbury Park, CA: Sage.

Kaufman, R. (1993a, March). Educational restructuring which will work: Beyond tinkering. *International Journal of Education Reform.*

Kaufman, R. (1993b, October). Mega planning: The argument is over. *Performance & Instruction.*

Kaufman, R. (1993c, April). The vision thing: Florida's salvation. *Ideas in Action*, 2(5).

Kaufman, R. (1994, April). A synergistic focus for educational quality management, needs assessment, and strategic planning. *International Journal of Education Reform*, 3(2), 174-180.

Kaufman, R. (1995). *Mapping educational success: Strategic thinking and planning for school administrators* (Rev. ed.). Thousand Oaks, CA: Corwin.

Kaufman, R., Grisé, P., & Watters, K. (1992a). Are our "needs" needs and are they important? In K. L. Medsker & D. G. Roberts (Eds.), *ASTD Trainer's toolkit: Evaluating the results of training.* Arlington, VA: American Society for Training & Development.

Kaufman, R., Grisé, P., & Watters, K. (1992b). Deriving a vision. In K. L. Medsker & D. G. Roberts (Eds.), *ASTD Trainer's toolkit: Evaluating the results of training.* Arlington, VA: American Society for Training & Development.

Kaufman, R., Grisé, P., & Watters, K. (1992c). Needs assessment summary forms. In K. L. Medsker & D. G. Roberts (Eds.), *ASTD Trainer's toolkit: Evaluating the results of training.* Arlington, VA: American Society for Training & Development.

Kaufman, R., Grisé, P., & Watters, K. (1992d). Preparing useful performance indicators. In K. L. Medsker & D. G. Roberts (Eds.), *ASTD Trainer's toolkit: Evaluating the results of training.* Arlington, VA: American Society for Training & Development.

Kaufman, R., Grisé, P., & Watters, K. (1992e). Selecting and getting agreement on the scope of needs assessment and/or strategic planning. In K. L. Medsker & D. G. Roberts (Eds.), *ASTD Trainer's toolkit: Evaluating the results of training.* Arlington, VA: American Society for Training & Development.

Kaufman, R., & Herman, J. (1991). *Strategic planning in education: Rethinking, restructuring, revitalizing.* Lancaster, PA: Technomic.

Kaufman, R., Herman, J., & Watters, K. (1995). *Educational planning: Operational, tactical.* Lancaster, PA: Technomic.

Kaufman, R., Rojas, A. M., & Mayer, H. (1993). *Needs assessment: A user's guide.* Englewood Cliffs, NJ: Educational Technology.

Kaufman, R., & Valentine, G. (1989, November-December). Relating needs assessment and needs analysis. *Performance & Instruction.*

Kaufman, R., & Watters, C. (1992). Future challenges to performance technology: Ethics, professionalism, quality. In *Performance Technology Handbook.* National Society for Performance & Instruction and Jossey-Bass.

Kaufman, R., & Zahn, D. (1993). *Quality management plus: The continuous improvement of education.* Newbury Park, CA: Corwin.

Kuhn, T. (1970). *The structure of scientific revolution* (2nd ed.). Chicago: University of Chicago Press.

94   AUDITING YOUR EDUCATIONAL STRATEGIC PLAN

Mager, R. F. (1975). *Preparing instructional objectives* (2nd ed.). Belmont, CA: Pitman Learning.

Mager, R. F. (1988). *Making instruction work: Or skillbloomers.* Belmont, CA: David S. Lake.

Marshall, R., & Tucker, M. (1992). *Thinking for a living: Education and the wealth of nations.* New York: Basic Books.

Martin, R. (1993, November-December). Changing the mind of the organization. *Harvard Business Review.*

Naisbitt, J., & Aburdene, P. (1990). *Megatrends 2000: Ten new directions for the 1990s.* New York: William Morrow.

Ohmae, K. (1982). *The mind of the strategist: Business planning for competitive advantage.* New York: Penguin.

Osborne, D., & Gaebler, T. (1992). *Reinventing government: How the entrepreneurial spirit is transforming the public sector.* Reading, MA: Addison-Wesley.

Peddiwell, J. A. (H. Benjamin). (1939). *The sabertooth curriculum.* New York: McGraw-Hill.

Perelman, L. J. (1989, November 28). *Closing education's technology gap* (Briefing Paper No. 111). Indianapolis, IN: Hudson Institute.

Perelman, L. J. (1990, May). *The "academia" deception* (Briefing Paper No. 120). Indianapolis, IN: Hudson Institute.

Peters, T. (1987). *Thriving on chaos: Handbook for a management revolution.* New York: Alfred A. Knopf.

Popcorn, F. (1991). *The Popcorn report.* New York: Doubleday.

Roberts, W. (1987). *Leadership secrets of Attila the Hun.* New York: Warner.

Roberts, W. (1991). *Straight A's never made anybody rich.* New York: HarperCollins.

Rummler, G. A., & Brache, A. P. (1990). *Improving performance: How to manage the white space on the organization chart.* San Francisco: Jossey-Bass.

Schlechty, P. C. (1990). *Schools for the 21st century: Leadership imperatives for educational reform.* San Francisco: Jossey-Bass.

Senge, P. M. (1990). *The fifth discipline: The art and practice of the learning organization.* New York: Doubleday-Currency.

Shanker, A. (1990, January). The end of the traditional model of schooling—And a proposal for using incentives to restructure public schools. *Phi Delta Kappan.*

Sobel, I., & Kaufman, R. (1989). Toward a "hard" metric for educational utility. *Performance Improvement Quarterly, 2*(1).

Stevens, S. (1946). On the theory of scales of measurement. *Science, 103.*

Stevens, S. (1951). *Handbook of experimental psychology.* New York: John Wiley.

Toffler, A. (1990). *Powershift: Knowledge, wealth, and violence at the edge of the 21st century.* New York: Bantam.

Windham, D. M. (1988). *Indicators of educational effectiveness and efficiency.* Tallahassee: Florida State University, Learning Systems Institute, IESS Educational Efficiency Clearinghouse (for the U.S. Agency for International Development, Bureau of Science and Technology, Office of Education).

Witkin, B. R. (1984). *Assessing needs in educational and social programs.* San Francisco: Jossey-Bass.

Witkin, B. R. (1991). Setting priorities: Needs assessment in time of change. In R. V. Carlson & G. Awkerman (Eds.), *Educational planning: Concepts, strategies, and practices.* New York: Longman.

Witkin, B. R. (1994). Needs assessment since 1981: The state of the practice. *Evaluation Practice, 15*(1), 17-27.

CORWIN
PRESS

The Corwin Press logo—a raven striding across an open book—represents the happy union of courage and learning. We are a professional-level publisher of books and journals for K-12 educators, and we are committed to creating and providing resources that embody these qualities. Corwin's motto is "Success for All Learners."